Houston Cooks ★

FRANCINE SPIERING

Houston Cooks

Recipes from the City's Favorite Restaurants and Chefs

Vancouver / Berkeley

To our fishers, farmers, and ranchers, who bring us good things to cook with. To the chefs who show us how.

★ ★ ★

Recipes are chef tested.

19 20 21 22 23 5 4 3 2 1

Cataloguing data is available from Library and Archives Canada
ISBN 978-1-77327-074-6 (hbk.)

Design by Naomi MacDougall
Photography by Chris Brown
Prop styling by Tina Hunt

Editing by Michelle Meade
Copy editing by Judy Phillips
Proofreading by Lucy Kenward
Indexing by Iva Cheung

Printed and bound in China by C&C Offset Printing Co., Ltd.
Distributed internationally by Publishers Group West

Figure 1 Publishing Inc.
Vancouver BC Canada
www.figure1publishing.com

Recipe Notes
Butter is unsalted.
All citrus juices are freshly squeezed.
Black pepper is freshly ground.
Fresh herbs are used throughout unless specified otherwise.

IMAGE ON PREVIOUS SPREAD:
Shrimp and Grits, p. 113

Contents

Introduction

★ ★ ★

Welcome to Houston. We're the Space City, the Bayou City, or simply H-Town. And we're big. Houston is the largest city in the South and Southwest, and the fourth most populous city in the U.S. An urban sprawl that ebbs into semirural areas as it spans across nine counties.

But take a closer look and you'll discover a fascinating and vibrant city that has both cosmopolitan allure and small-town charm. It's a city with leading performing arts, a walkable museum district, landmark street art, and myriad restaurants, bars, and microbreweries. And just a stone's throw from downtown are quaint neighborhoods, urban vegetable farms, and community gardens.

Although oil and gas is a major industry here, another wave of energy is grabbing attention. Houston has been invigorated by a cultural and community dynamism, a new thinking that welcomes creative impulse and innovation and that acknowledges the need to preserve the heritage and habitat of our urban bounds (and beyond). As a result, the landscape is changing, both literally and expressively.

Our downtown, for instance, has seen massive improvements in recent years, transforming it from a concrete jungle to a happening heart of the city. An eyesore of a parking lot has been replaced with Discovery Green, a twelve-acre, certified-sustainable park hosting free events, from yoga classes to movie nights. Historic sites that lay dormant for decades were cleaned up and revitalized, including Allen's Landing, where Augustus Chapman Allen and John Kirby Allen first set foot and founded Houston. Many of the historic buildings around the stroll-worthy area of Market Square and Main Street have been restored to their former glory, now housing bars, restaurants, and (most excitingly) newly developed upscale food halls. The Arts District, encompassing Houston's oldest neighborhoods, was reimagined as the vibrant soul of Houston's art scene in repurposed warehouses and former silos. The same level of urban transformation is spreading to Midtown, EaDo (East Downtown), and north to what is now the Warehouse District.

At the same time, we wised up to the need to preserve our natural surroundings. There's Coastal Prairie Partnership, which strives to conserve and restore coastal prairie ecosystems (including pockets of prairie in the city); the Buffalo Bayou Partnership, which zooms in on the 10-mile stretch of Houston's iconic river that runs through downtown; and the Galveston Bay Foundation, which works to protect, preserve, and conserve the area and its wildlife, shores, and wetlands.

Nature has a place in urban growth, not least because a healthy outdoor environment allows for a local food system to thrive. We get fresh seafood from Galveston Bay—large, plump, naturally sweet and juicy shrimp, sweet-briny oysters, delicate blue crabs—and access to Texas quail, venison from the Hill Country, pasture-raised poultry, and grass-fed beef. In winter, trees here are heavy with an abundant variety of citrus, including satsuma, kumquat, grapefruit, and all kinds of oranges. Summer is for eggplant, okra, peaches, and hot peppers. And we can forage numerous edible mushrooms, nuts, fruits, and greens in the nature parks and forests in and around Houston.

Local farmers and producers are gaining a stronger foothold in the city. They supply citywide farmers' markets, restaurants, and grocery stores with meats, dairy, and eggs, and just-harvested vegetables, fruits, and herbs. They provide us with exciting artisanal products like goat milk gelato, wild boar chorizo, and authentic Italian cheese made with Texas dairy. It is a bounty that completes the world of local flavors you will find in Houston, created by the people of our food community.

The seven sculptures at Buffalo Bayou Park known collectively as Tolerance represent and symbolize both cultural acceptance and unification. Houston takes pride in its wide-open arms, and the immigrants who've settled here have enriched our cultural and culinary landscape. With over 145 languages spoken here, it's no wonder that Houston is one of the most ethnically diverse cities in the U.S. Translate that into cuisines, and that's a gastronomic world tour within the city limits.

Drive out to East End for steamed tamales and freshly made tortillas at a family-owned tortilleria. Head to Hillcroft and shop for an Indian spice box, khoya, or syrupy pastries galore. Or to Bellaire Boulevard, where just west of the Beltway street names are written in Vietnamese and supermarkets sell everything from Southeast Asian herbs and spices to woks and clay pots. The city is dotted with international supermarkets, where you'll find whatever you need, including all the ingredients you come across in this book, from ancho chile to tahini, honeycomb tripe to crawfish tails. And let's not forget our cultural events. There's a festival for just about any food and cuisine found in this city, from pierogi at the Polish festival to pide at Turk-Fest and bulgogi at the Korean festival.

Our city is a proud and colorful culinary tapestry, a conflation of gastronomic diversity and local and international food traditions. Take barbecue, for instance. We've always queued up for 'cue, but more recently, Houston's barbecue scene has been bolder than ever with global flavors, along with an awareness and sourcing of responsibly raised meats. We boast an extraordinary cross-pollination of styles and cultures, and it's the norm now to find Mexican, Italian, Vietnamese (and everything in between) mixed in with Gulf

Coast traditions, seasonality, and locally sourced ingredients on the menu. We have an amazing food community of independent chefs, restaurateurs, bartenders, and artisans who believe in their craft and inspire us. They push boundaries, they take risks, and, best of all, deliver. In turn, they can count on an appreciative dining audience. Houstonians have an insatiable appetite for good food, and collectively, we are always craving variety.

Each of the featured chefs in this book brings a unique taste of Houston. The profiles offer insight into the lives of our chefs, who work tirelessly to make our dining scene so exciting. You will discover their ambitions and inspiration, and the roots of their culinary philosophies. Their dishes are defined by food provenance (such as charred eggplant and okra with burrata; see page 198), heritage (such as traditional Japanese cured fish; see

page 195), or fond childhood memories (such as Thit Kho Tàu; see page 185).

Houston has been firmly marked as one of America's best dining destinations, and I can understand why. We have mouthwatering diversity. We find abundant fresh ingredients at our fingertips. We prepare food with deft hands. And we give meaning to the belief that food brings people together. I hope that, as Houston continues to expand, we continue to preserve its heritage and nurture the core energy of culture that gives the city its character.

Now, let's turn these pages and taste Houston.

Second Servings of Houston

★ ★ ★

Houston Cooks celebrates the city's thriving food scene. But as we do (and proudly so), we are also cognizant of the fact that not everyone can afford to sit at the proverbial table. In fact, one in five Houstonians face food insecurity on a daily basis, and rely on the nonprofits that work hard to create a safety net for those who need it.

Second Servings of Houston is a nonprofit that connects the dots between food insecurity and avoidable food waste. Since 2014, it has rescued over two million pounds of food (valued at over 10 million dollars), and each year, it provides wholesome food to 135,000 people in need.

The nonprofit picks up perishable food that has been left unserved or unsold from hotels, sports venues, and food retail outlets and delivers it the very same day to approved charity sites, including local shelters, soup kitchens, and low-income housing.

"You have food insecurity on one hand and, on the other, 30 percent to 40 percent food waste at the retail and consumer level. Food rescue makes so much sense, because it is a practical and efficient approach to both pressing issues," explains founder and CEO Barbara Bronstein.

To increase its reach and effectiveness, Second Servings is constantly developing new initiatives and programs. The organization offers training to the charity centers' cooks, who learn to prepare healthy menus with fresh produce donations. "Sharing baskets" at public schools allow children and teachers to enjoy intact fruit.

Second Servings is a prominent resource against hunger and waste in Houston, and a portion of proceeds from book sales of *Houston Cooks* will be donated to its cause. For more information, please visit www.secondservingshouston.org.

The Restaurants

The Recipes

Atlas Diner HTX

RICHARD KNIGHT

★ Chef Richard Knight is indubitably Houston's uncrowned king of nose-to-tail cooking. At a time when the culinary wealth of offal meats (and Gulf bycatch, by the way) remained largely unexplored by his peers, he was serving up blood sausage, pickled lamb tongues, and pork-cheek salad at his restaurant Feast, back in 2008.

The James Beard Award–nominated chef is loved for his scrumptious food rooted in his native British cuisine and a signature quirk—from an elephant teapot as a vessel for a sauce to his signature chicken liver mousse cones sprinkled with candy-colored fennel seeds (page 18).

At Atlas Diner HTX (located in Bravery Chef Hall), Knight puts his idiosyncratic spin on vintage American diner culture—starting with a painting on the wall of four pigs in an Edward Hopper–esque diner scene, wittily named *Night Hogs at the Diner*. The menu offerings include Countryside Farm's rabbit and white bean chimichanga, generously sauced with lamb-chorizo gravy; thick Japanese soufflé pancakes dressed with sausage, pineapple, egg, and pork syrup; and egg salad rolls fully loaded with sweet and spicy jalapeño, radishes, and smoky paprika. And check out the goat-cheese cheesecake made with Blue Heron Farm's feta and fresh berries, created by his wife, Carrie.

A commitment to local farmers is in the chef's gastronomic DNA. In fact, he's taken his advocacy beyond the kitchen door in the documentary series *Show Us Your Goods*, in which he and Carrie visit local ranchers, artisans, and food-industry leaders who support sustainable farming, animal welfare, cooking, and culture. Together, they prepare meals and break bread, celebrating those who impact the food community.

Now, how much fun would it be to watch that documentary series while pigging out at the diner? "One day soon, you just might," suggests Knight.

2 whole chickens, thoroughly washed and dried

4 red onions, peeled and roots cut off

Olive oil, for brushing and drizzling

Salt and black pepper

4 sprigs thyme

1 head Romaine lettuce, leaves separated and chopped

3 radishes, thinly sliced

½ bunch Italian parsley, leaves only

3 Tbsp sherry vinegar

Chicken Onion

SERVES 4 With this dish, chef Richard Knight shows us that even a humble onion can be the star on a plate. Ask your butcher to remove the skin from the chicken or follow the instructions below. Alternatively, use bacon strips instead of chicken skin, for a different flavor.

Place chickens on a cutting board breast side up. Using a sharp knife, cut through the skin on one side of the breastbone, from the neck down to the end where the breastbone meets the cavity.

Still working on the one side of the breastbone, gently push your thumbs under the skin and carefully peel back the skin, keeping it in one piece if possible. When you get to the leg, continue pulling off the skin. Cut the skin at the end of the leg so it slides off. Repeat on the other side of the chicken. Then repeat with the second chicken. (Save the chickens for another dish, perhaps freezing for future use.)

Preheat oven to 300°F.

Cut a ½-inch-deep cross at the top of each onion. Cut 4 pieces of foil, large enough to loosely wrap each onion.

Using a pastry brush, generously brush oil on one side of each piece of foil, then place an onion, root side down, in the center of each oiled side. Season generously with salt and pepper, and top each with a thyme sprig. Wrap onions in chicken skin. Carefully fold up the corners of the foil so that the onion is just sealed but the sides of the foil are not touching the chicken skin. Place on a baking sheet and bake for 1 to 2 hours, until onions are soft yet still have a little body.

Remove chicken onions from foil, reserving the juices. Place chicken onions on the baking sheet and drizzle with olive oil. Season each with a pinch of salt.

Increase oven temperature to 450°F. Roast chicken onions for 3 to 5 minutes, until the skin is crispy.

In a bowl, mix together lettuce, radishes, and parsley. Reserve 1 cup for garnish. Pour the reserved cooled chicken juices into a small bowl, whisk in vinegar, taste for seasoning, and pour over salad. Toss and divide among four plates. Carefully place the chicken onions on the salad and serve immediately.

Chicken liver mousse

1¼ cups (2½ sticks) butter

1 lb chicken livers

1 Tbsp thyme leaves or chervil

1 tsp kosher salt

¾ tsp garlic powder

¾ tsp onion powder

¼ tsp celery salt

¼ tsp cayenne pepper

⅛ tsp pink curing salt (see Note)

2 medium eggs

¼ cup heavy cream

Sherry syrup

¼ cup sherry

¼ cup sugar

Assembly

20 ice-cream cones

1 cup candied fennel seeds (see Note)

½ cup chopped chervil, parsley, or chives, for garnish

Maldon sea salt, for finishing

Note: Pink curing salt, also known as pink salt, is used to kill undesirable bacteria and makes mousses like this safe to eat. The salt also helps stabilize the color. Curing salt is toxic in large doses and should not be sprinkled directly on food.

Sugar-coated fennel seeds (*meethi saunf*) are often consumed at the end of an Indian meal to sweeten the breath, cleanse the palate, and aid digestion.

Chicken Liver Mousse

MAKES 20 Looking for an appetizer dish with a wow factor? These miniature cones are filled with rich buttery mousse, drizzled with sherry syrup, and dotted with candied fennel. The mousse can be stored in the freezer for 3 months at least. When ready to serve, simply allow it to defrost in the refrigerator and then bring it to room temperature. Have leftovers? Slather the mousse onto crusty bread any time you crave it.

Chicken liver mousse Melt butter in a small saucepan over low heat, allowing the solids to rise to the surface and separate from the clear fat. Strain through a sieve lined with cheesecloth or coffee filter over a small bowl. Set this clarified butter aside.

Prepare a double boiler with the hot water ready in the lower pan, and set aside a large bowl of ice water. (You will need to work fast once the mousse mixture is cooked to prevent discoloration.)

Wash and dry the livers well. Remove any tough membranes. Transfer the livers to a blender, then add thyme (or chervil), seasonings, eggs, and clarified butter. Purée until smooth. Using a rubber spatula, scrape mixture into the top pan of the double boiler and set over the bottom pan. Cook over medium heat, gently stirring the mousse and scraping the sides of the pan occasionally (for even cooking), for 8 to 10 minutes, or until the temperature reaches 165°F.

Remove the double boiler from the heat and immediately scrape mixture into a fine-mesh sieve set over a deep bowl. Using a rubber spatula, push the mixture through the sieve. Using an immersion blender, quickly mix in the cream. Cover with plastic wrap, making sure it touches the entire surface of the mousse (to prevent discoloration). Place the bowl in the ice-water bath, then let cool completely in the refrigerator.

Sherry syrup Combine sherry and sugar in a small saucepan and bring to a boil over medium-high heat. Reduce heat to medium, then simmer for 5 to 10 minutes, until syrupy. Let cool.

Assembly Using a serrated knife, carefully cut the cones about 2 inches from the bottom tip, to create miniature cones.

Place the miniature cones in small bowls or glasses. Transfer mousse into a piping bag fitted with a large star tip. Pipe mousse into each cone, swirling it on top. Finish each with a drop of sherry syrup, candied fennel, and herbs. Add a touch of sea salt and serve immediately.

B&B Butchers & Restaurant

TOMMY ELBASHARY

★ The once-abandoned redbrick building on Washington Avenue was done justice when proprietor Benjamin Berg restored it in 2014. He preserved the original wooden beams, exposed the interior brickwork and steel columns, and opened up the space. And with an artisanal butcher shop, and a meat cellar full of dry-aged cuts, Berg brought a touch of Manhattan's Meatpacking District to Houston's First Ward.

On a balmy night, nothing beats sitting at a table out on the airy patio. Start with a B&B Bellini and crackling-crisp house-smoked bacon, and peruse the menu. Meat is king here but it rules alongside delectable seafood, from a raw-bar shellfish tower to pan-seared Dover sole with brown butter.

Chief Executive Chef Tommy Elbashary brings more than thirty-two years of experience to the butcher block. He describes his steakhouse's menu as an "encyclopedia of steaks," the chef's way of saying he's proud of the variety of steaks, different grades, and cattle breeds the restaurant offers. Its most prized A5 Kobe beef is valued for its speckled marbling and comes from the rare 100 percent *Tajima-gyu* (Japanese black) cattle raised in Hyogo Valley near Kobe, Japan. In fact, B&B Butchers is one of only ten restaurants in the U.S. to sell this premium cut.

The twelve-course tasting menu is a carnivore's delight. Curated by Elbashary and presented by Berg, guests taste and compare exclusive cellar cuts, including twenty-eight-day and fifty-five-day dry-aged Texas and Japanese wagyu and A5 Kobe. It's the perfect way to sample Elbashary's "encyclopedia" of steak.

Whole-grain mustard sauce

1 Tbsp butter

1 Tbsp finely chopped shallots

¼ cup white wine

1 cup heavy cream

2 Tbsp whole-grain mustard

Salt and black pepper

Crab cakes

¼ cup mayonnaise

½ Tbsp Old Bay seasoning

1 egg yolk

1 lb jumbo lump crabmeat, shells picked

1 Tbsp chopped chives

1 cup crushed cornflakes

Chopped Italian parsley, for garnish (optional)

Crab Cakes with Whole-Grain Mustard Sauce

SERVES 4 These lavish crab cakes require minimal effort for maximum results. At B&B Butchers & Restaurant, copious nubbins of crabmeat are delicately bound with an egg yolk and a little mayonnaise and finished with a light-as-air cornflake crunch. The best crabmeat for these irresistible bundles is sold as jumbo lump and comes from the legs of larger crabs.

Whole-grain mustard sauce Melt butter in a medium saucepan over medium-high heat. Add shallots and sauté for 2 minutes or until translucent.

Pour in wine and cook for 1 to 2 minutes, until reduced by half. Pour in cream and cook for another 5 minutes or until sauce is thick enough to coat the back of a wooden spoon. Stir in mustard and season with salt and pepper.

Crab cakes Preheat oven to 300°F.

In a large bowl, combine mayonnaise and Old Bay seasoning. Add egg yolk and mix well. Using a spoon, gently fold in crabmeat and chives. Divide the crab mixture into 4 portions and, using your hands, shape each into a ball. Pat down gently to form 2-inch-thick patties.

Put cornflakes into a wide bowl. Carefully dredge the crab cakes in the cornflakes to coat all sides. Place crab cakes on a baking sheet and bake for 10 to 15 minutes, until golden brown.

Assembly Spoon 2 tablespoons of sauce on each of four plates. Carefully place a crab cake on top of the sauce. Garnish with parsley, if using, and serve immediately.

Duxelle

1 Tbsp butter

2 shallots, finely chopped

1 clove garlic, finely chopped

Salt and black pepper

8 oz cremini mushrooms, chopped

8 oz white button mushrooms, chopped

8 oz oyster mushrooms, chopped

½ cup Marsala

½ cup panko breadcrumbs

1 Tbsp chopped Italian parsley

½ Tbsp chopped thyme

Beef Wellington

1 (2- to 2½-lb) center-cut beef tenderloin

Salt and black pepper

1 Tbsp olive oil

1 Tbsp butter

½ lb foie gras (preferably Hudson Valley), cut into ¼-inch-thick slices

2 store-bought crepes (or a 10- × 15-inch sheet of filo pastry)

Duxelle (see here)

1 (10- × 15-inch) sheet frozen puff pastry

1 large egg, beaten

Beef Wellington with Madeira Sauce

SERVES 4 TO 6 Beef Wellington is an impressive centerpiece for special occasions, and this recipe is no exception. The chef prepares individual portions, but we've presented the recipe family-style. The layer of crepes (filo pastry also works) between the meat prevents the pastry from becoming too soggy. Foie gras can be ordered online at D'artagnan or in advance at Central Market. Alternatively, use pâté de foie gras or creamy chicken liver pâté.

Duxelle Melt butter in a frying pan over medium-high heat. Add shallots, garlic, salt, and pepper, reduce heat to medium, and cook for 2 to 3 minutes, until shallots are translucent. Add mushrooms and sauté for 5 to 7 minutes, until tender. Increase heat to medium-high, pour in Marsala, and cook for another 2 to 3 minutes, until most of the Marsala has evaporated. Set aside to cool.

Transfer mixture to a food processor and add panko breadcrumbs, parsley, and thyme. Process to a coarse purée. Set aside.

Beef Wellington Preheat oven to 400°F. Generously season tenderloin with salt and pepper.

Heat oil and butter in a large frying pan over medium-high heat. Add tenderloin and sear for 1 minute on each side. Use kitchen tongs to handle the tenderloin when searing the top and bottom end. Set aside to cool.

In the same pan set over high heat, sear foie gras for 30 seconds. Flip and sear for another 30 seconds. Set aside.

On a clean work surface, lay out crepes (or filo pastry) and overlap to form a 10- × 15-inch "blanket." Spread out the duxelle in a layer to cover the crepe surface. Place the tenderloin at one end and arrange the foie gras on top. Roll up the tenderloin in the crepe, making sure the foie gras ends up on top. Cut excess crepe off the outer ends and tuck under to close. Wrap tightly in plastic wrap (like a sausage) and chill in the refrigerator for 30 minutes.

Lay the puff pastry on the work surface. Remove the plastic from the tenderloin and place the tenderloin on the pastry. Brush egg wash along the edges of the puff pastry. Fold pastry over to cover completely, tuck in the ends, and trim off

Madeira sauce

1 Tbsp butter

1 large shallot, chopped

2 cloves garlic, chopped

1 tsp cracked black
    peppercorns

1 bay leaf

Sprig of thyme

2 cups demi-glace
    (see Note), beef stock,
    or veal stock

1 cup Madeira wine

1 Tbsp cornstarch
    dissolved in 1 Tbsp
    water (optional)

Salt and black pepper

any excess. The foie gras side should face up. Chill for 30 minutes to relax the gluten and minimize shrinkage during baking.

Preheat oven to 400°F.

Brush top of pastry with egg wash, then lightly score it, taking care not to cut all the way through. Place on a baking sheet and roast for 30 to 40 minutes, until the tenderloin is medium-rare. (Or when the internal temperature reaches 135°F on an instant-read thermometer.)

Madeira sauce Melt butter in a saucepan over medium heat. Add shallot and garlic and sauté for 2 minutes. Add peppercorns, bay leaf, and thyme and sauté for another minute. Increase heat to medium-high, pour in Madeira, and cook for another 2 to 3 minutes, until reduced by half.

Pour in demi-glace (or stock) and cook for another 2 to 3 minutes, until reduced by a third. (If you use stock, you can thicken the sauce with the cornstarch mixture. Add the mixture to the sauce, a little at a time, until thickened to your desired consistency.) Season with salt and pepper. Strain and keep warm.

Assembly Remove the Wellington from the oven and let rest for 10 to 15 minutes. Using a serrated knife, cut the Wellington into thick slices and serve with Madeira sauce.

Note: Demi-glace (veal glaze) is a gourmet item that can be found at fine food stores, Central Market, or via Amazon. Alternatively, use a good-quality beef stock and thicken with a little cornstarch.

Beef Wellington with Madeira Sauce | p. 22–23

B.B. Italia Kitchen & Bar

DANIEL BERG

Daniel Berg
Executive Chef

★ When Carmelo Mauro closed his namesake restaurant in late 2017 (after thirty-eight years of operation), fans of the classic Italian stalwart shed collective tears. That is, until Berg Hospitality's restaurateur Benjamin Berg announced he would take over and resurrect it. Even bigger smiles broke out when Benjamin's brother Daniel—whose fine-dining pedigree traces back to Michelin-starred restaurants in Milan and Sicily—flew in from New York to helm the kitchen. "I came here to work with my brother," Daniel shares. The two brothers hadn't lived in the same city in almost twenty years.

The name change to B.B. Italia Kitchen & Bar in early 2019 was a prelude to a complete overhaul of the outdated building, inside and out. The Berg brothers opened up a patio, added a wine room, expanded the bar area, and created an appealing environment for diners to come together in and have a great meal.

Italian-American cuisine is in the chef's blood and bones. "I love cooking this type of food because it reminds me of my childhood," Berg says, reminiscing about home-cooked meals at friends' houses, and the classic "red sauce" he grew up eating at Italian restaurants in New York City.

B.B. Italia offers Italian-American cuisine continued in that New York tradition, and classics such as veal piccata, eggplant parmigiana, and chicken Marsala (page 28) endure. "Everything, including our pastas, is made fresh in-house," says Daniel. This is finely tuned comfort food: ravioli stuffed with short rib, strozzapreti nestled in basil pesto, and bucatini tossed with black olives, capers, and anchovies. One of the big advantages of being in the Berg Hospitality Group? That hefty *bistecca Fiorentina*, a thick-cut dry-aged porterhouse cooked rare, is sourced from B&B Butchers. It's a win-win for us diners all around.

▶ Chicken Marsala | p. 28

4 skinless, boneless
  chicken breasts
Salt and pepper
1 Tbsp butter
1 Tbsp olive oil
1 large shallot, thinly sliced
1 lb cremini mushrooms,
  sliced
1 cup Marsala wine
Sprig of rosemary
Sprig of thyme

2 cups demi-glace
  (see Note)
1 cup heavy cream
2 cups wilted spinach,
  to serve (optional)
½ cup chopped Italian
  parsley, for garnish

Note: Demi-glace (veal glaze) is a gourmet item
that can be found at fine food stores, Central
Market, or via Amazon. Alternatively, use a
good-quality beef stock and thicken with a little
cornstarch.

Chicken Marsala

SERVES 4 This classic dish of chicken breast swaddled in a glossy, Marsala-scented creamy mushroom sauce is homey and elegant at the same time. At B.B. Italia Kitchen & Bar, the sauce is made with demi-glace, a rich brown sauce frequently used in French cuisine as the basis for other sauces.

Put a chicken breast on a cutting board and place a sheet of plastic wrap on top. Using a meat mallet (or rolling pin), gently pound chicken to a ½-inch thickness. Start at the center of the breast and work outward to avoid breaking the meat around the edges. Repeat with the remaining chicken.

Season chicken breasts with salt and pepper. Heat butter in a large frying pan over medium-high heat. Add chicken and cook for 5 minutes. Flip over and cook for another 5 minutes. Transfer to a plate and set aside.

Heat oil in the same frying pan over medium heat. Add shallot and cook for 3 minutes or until tender and translucent. Add mushrooms and cook for 2 minutes or until they start to soften and color. Pour in Marsala, increase heat to medium-high, and cook for 2 minutes or until reduced by half.

Tie together thyme and rosemary with a piece of kitchen string. Add demi-glace, cream, and herb bundle to the pan and bring mixture to a boil. Reduce heat to medium-low and simmer for 10 minutes. Remove herbs. Add chicken and cook for another 5 minutes.

Arrange a bed of wilted spinach, if using, on a serving dish. Add the chicken Marsala and mushrooms on top, garnish with parsley, and serve family-style.

4 cups heavy cream

4 cups tomato passata

2 Tbsp chili flakes

Salt and pepper

1 Tbsp olive oil

2 large yellow onions, chopped

8 slices applewood-smoked bacon, diced

2 to 3 cloves garlic, finely chopped

1 cup vodka (optional)

2 lbs dried rigatoni

2 to 4 Tbsp butter

¼ cup chopped basil, for garnish

¼ cup chopped Italian parsley, for garnish

Grated Parmesan, for sprinkling

Rigatoni alla Vodka

SERVES 8 Rigatoni alla vodka is an Italian-American classic, with or without the vodka! At B.B. Italia Kitchen & Bar the flavor is built with bacon, garlic, chili flakes, and, of course, tomatoes. If adding vodka to this recipe, be sure to cook out the alcohol completely. The killer sauce can be served with your favorite pasta and will leave you wanting for nothing—except perhaps a small side salad and extra Parmesan on top.

Heat cream in a large saucepan over medium heat for 10 to 15 minutes, until reduced by half. Add passata, chili flakes, salt, and pepper. Reduce heat to low and stir for 3 to 4 minutes.

Heat oil in a wide saucepan over medium-low heat. Add onions and bacon and cook for 10 minutes or until onions are softened and caramelized. Add garlic and cook for another minute. Pour in vodka, if using, and cook for 2 to 3 minutes, until reduced by half. Add the onion mixture (with the bacon fat) to the tomato-cream sauce and bring to a gentle boil over medium heat. Reduce heat to medium-low and simmer for 15 minutes. Keep warm.

Meanwhile, in a large saucepan of boiling salted water, cook rigatoni according to the package directions until al dente. Drain pasta.

Stir butter into the sauce, add pasta, and mix well. Serve family-style in a large serving bowl. Finish with basil, parsley, and Parmesan and serve immediately.

Brasserie 19

JAIME SALAZAR

⭐ The best way to start your meal at this brasserie is with an aperitif at the long bar, watching oysters being shucked to order.

Located in the heart of River Oaks, Brasserie 19 became an instant classic the moment it opened, in 2011. It's a simple yet elegant space, informed by detail. The warmly lit dining room—with a pale gray tufted banquette along one side of the room, mirrors on a paneled wall, and handsome chevron wood floors—is effortlessly chic.

Refinement is expressed throughout the menu too: a crispy frisée salad is loaded with lardons and croutons and topped with a perfectly poached egg; tender escargots are bathed in hot garlic butter, and steak tartare is seasoned to perfection. Combine that with an attractive (and attractively priced) wine list, and wining and dining here can't help but be a classy French affair.

Chef Jaime Salazar is in his element cooking French cuisine. "It's a market-driven cuisine," he says. "And we like to keep things fresh and simple." He mentions the market fish—a pan-seared Gulf fish drizzled with *sauce vierge* (a French sauce made with olive oil, lemon juice, tomato, and basil). Salazar then gets lyrical as he talks about the house-made charcuterie, French garlic sausage, and shredded duck confit, which is made with aromatic duck fat, mustard, and parsley for rillettes.

Salazar was first introduced to classic French cuisine when his godmother took him to Paris and surprised him by taking him to a demo class at Le Cordon Bleu. That was in 2004, and he was just sixteen years old. After graduating from culinary school in Las Vegas and dedicating a few years on the line at Clark Cooper Concepts, Salazar is bringing a taste of Paris to his home turf.

Seafood stock

1½ lbs head-on shrimp

1 (2-lb) lobster

2 Tbsp olive oil

4 carrots, peeled and cut
   into ½-inch pieces

4 stalks celery, cut into
   ½-inch pieces

3 white onions, chopped

1 bay leaf

1 Tbsp tomato paste

1 cup white wine

1 lb white fish bones

Bouillabaisse

SERVES 6 Bouillabaisse, a seafood stew that originated in Marseille, France, was traditionally prepared by fishers who needed to use up whatever catch they could not sell. Over time, more refined versions emerged around the world, reflecting local seafood and other regional ingredients. Brasserie 19's bouillabaisse sees fresh seafood in an aromatic broth. The double stock extracts every last bit of flavor from the fish bones and seafood shells.

Seafood stock Peel shrimp, reserving heads and shells in a large bowl. Put shrimp in a bowl, cover, and refrigerate until needed.

To prepare the lobster, crack through the head lengthwise using a sharp chef's knife. Remove the meat from the claws and tail (reserve for later) and add the shells and head to the bowl of shrimp shells.

Heat oil in a large stockpot over medium-high heat. Add all shells and heads and cook for 3 minutes. Using a wooden spoon or metal potato masher, pound the shells gently but firmly to break them up (this will release flavor into the stock).

Add carrots, celery, onions, and bay leaf and sauté for 5 minutes over medium-low heat. Stir in tomato paste and cook for 1 minute.

Increase heat to high and pour in wine. Using a wooden spoon, scrape any browned bits off the bottom of the pan, then cook for 5 minutes or until the wine has nearly evaporated.

Add fish bones and 2½ quarts water and bring to a boil. Reduce heat to low, cover, and simmer for 1 hour. Set aside to cool, then strain stock into a large saucepan and press the back of a ladle against the shells to extract all the liquid. Set liquid aside. (Makes 2½ quarts.) Reserve 2 cups for mussels. (Stock can be stored in the refrigerator for up to 3 days or frozen for up to 1 month.)

Bouillabaisse stock

1 Tbsp olive oil

1 large onion, sliced

Stalks and core of 2 fennel bulbs, chopped

1 Tbsp tomato paste

½ cup Pernod

2 qts Seafood Stock (see here)

Juice and peel of 2 small oranges

Juice and peel of 2 lemons

2 sprigs tarragon

Pinch of saffron

Sea salt

Bouillabaisse

2 cups Seafood Stock (see here)

1 lb live mussels, scrubbed clean, debearded, and rinsed well

1 Tbsp olive oil

1 large yellow onion, thinly sliced

1 fennel bulb, thinly sliced

2 qts Bouillabaisse Stock (see here)

Reserved lobster meat, cut into bite-size chunks

Reserved raw shrimp

1 lb white fish or snapper, cut into 2-inch pieces

1 Tbsp thinly sliced basil, plus extra for garnish

1 lb raw sea scallops

Juice of 1 lemon

Sea salt and black pepper

1 lemon, cut into wedges, for serving

Bouillabaisse stock Heat oil in a stockpot over medium-high heat. Add onion and fennel stalks and core, lower heat to medium, and sauté for 8 to 10 minutes, until caramelized. Add tomato paste and cook for 1 minute.

Pour in Pernod and cook on high heat until reduced by half. Add seafood stock, orange and lemon juices and peels, tarragon, and saffron. Bring to a boil, then reduce heat to medium-low and cook, uncovered, for 30 minutes.

Season with salt. Strain stock into a large bowl and set aside.

Assembly Bring 2 cups seafood stock to a boil in a large saucepan on medium heat. Discard any mussels that are broken or do not shut when tapped. Add mussels, cover, and cook for 5 minutes. Using a slotted spoon, transfer mussels to a bowl and discard any that have not opened.

Heat oil in a large saucepan over medium-high heat. Add onion and fennel and sauté for 5 minutes. Add bouillabaisse stock and bring to a boil. Reduce heat to medium and add lobster, shrimp, fish, and basil. Simmer, uncovered, for 2 minutes. Add scallops and mussels (in their shells) and cook, uncovered, for another 2 minutes. Finish with lemon juice and season with salt and pepper.

Spoon seafood and fennel into individual bowls, then ladle in hot broth. Alternatively, serve family-style in a tureen. Garnish with basil and serve with lemon wedges.

Crepe batter

1 cup all-purpose flour

2 large eggs

1 cup whole milk

¼ cup (½ stick) butter, melted

Strawberries and rhubarb

1 lb strawberries, cut into bite-size pieces

2 stalks rhubarb, cut into ¼-inch-thick slices

1 cup granulated sugar

Black pepper mascarpone

1 heaping cup mascarpone

¼ cup confectioners' sugar

1 Tbsp black pepper

1 vanilla bean, halved lengthwise

Rhubarb-Strawberry Crepes with Black Pepper Mascarpone

SERVES 4 TO 6 The sweetness of the strawberries and bite of black pepper in the creamy mascarpone heighten the flavor (trust me) and make this a truly indulgent dessert. If you plan on making this dish frequently (and I suspect you will), consider investing in a crepe spreader. This tool has a wooden roller attached to the end of a stick, which allows you to thinly spread out batter. It's inexpensive and can be found at most cookware shops.

Crepe batter In a bowl, whisk together flour and eggs. Add milk and ¼ cup water and stir to combine. Mix in butter, then let sit at room temperature for at least 30 minutes.

In a small nonstick frying pan set over medium-low heat, add ⅓ cup batter and tilt the pan in a circular motion so the batter evenly and thinly coats the bottom. (Alternatively, use a crepe spreader, if you want the crepes really thin.) Cook for 2 minutes.

Using a spatula, flip the crepe and cook for another 30 seconds. Transfer to a plate and repeat with the remaining batter. Set crepes aside to cool.

Strawberries and rhubarb Place all ingredients in a medium saucepan and stir in ½ cup water. Bring to a boil, then reduce heat to low and simmer for 5 minutes, stirring occasionally, until strawberries and rhubarb have softened but not fully disintegrated. Let sit for 5 minutes and then strain. Set compote aside and reserve the strained liquid.

In a blender or food processor, blend a quarter of the compote and all the reserved liquid to form a smooth and syrupy purée. Set aside to cool.

Black pepper mascarpone In a stand mixer fitted with the whisk attachment, combine mascarpone, sugar, and pepper. Scrape in vanilla seeds and whisk for 2 minutes on high speed.

Assembly Preheat oven to 400°F. Line a baking sheet with parchment paper.

Spread 2 tablespoons compote on each crepe. Fold crepes in half, then in half again so each becomes a wedge of a crepe. Place filled crepes on the prepared baking sheet and bake for 4 to 5 minutes.

Using a wide spatula, carefully transfer crepes to individual plates. Garnish with a spoonful each of compote and purée. Add 2 to 3 dollops of black pepper mascarpone on top of each and dust with confectioners' sugar. Serve immediately.

Broken Barrel

HILDA YSUSI

⭐ Hughes Landing in The Woodlands got a lot more exciting when Hilda Ysusi opened Broken Barrel. This independent restaurant on the waterfront has a contemporary industrial vibe, heightened by the glass-paned garage door that pulls up to open onto the patio when the weather is nice. Yet it is Ysusi's food that garners the most attention.

Ysusi enjoys crossing borders in her kitchen: arancini is prepared with paella and served with Romesco sauce; creamy risotto is piled high with roasted jalapeño and crispy plantains. "I like to combine the traditional with something unexpected," says Ysusi, who often draws inspiration from her travels or ingredients new to her. She enjoys cooking in her open kitchen and interacting with her guests. In fact, her monthly Chef's Table is an up-close-and-personal cooking event that allows you to see the chef in action as she prepares a five-course meal in front of you.

Born and raised in Mexico City, Ysusi also infuses some of her native flavors into the dishes: roasted hominy is paired with dates and poppy-seed dressing in a pozole salad, while pulled duck in hoisin sauce is served with crispy tortillas and Asian pickled vegetables, for China-meets-Mexico duck tostadas.

With a wine certificate under her belt, Ysusi curates the wine list, offering two flights (one red, one white) that change regularly. In fact, she does wine dinners to challenge herself. "I choose the wine first, then decide on the food," she reveals. In fact, she will prepare two completely different dishes, then pair them with the same wine to show off its versatility. Needless to say, Ysusi's wine dinners are something to sign up for—it's where she shines most radiantly.

▶ **Benedict Rancheros with Corn Tortillas** | p. 38–39

Charred salsa

6 Roma tomatoes

¼ white onion

1 jalapeño pepper

2 cloves garlic

¼ bunch cilantro

2 Tbsp extra-virgin olive oil

2 tsp salt

Refried beans

1 Tbsp olive oil

¼ white onion, finely chopped

1 clove garlic, finely chopped

1 cup cooked black beans, mashed

Salt

Tortillas

2 cups masa harina (preferably Maseca)

1 tsp lard or vegetable oil

2 tsp salt

Benedict Rancheros with Corn Tortillas

SERVES 4 When a perfectly poached egg yolk runs into burnt-red salsa and spreads over the crisp edges of a homemade tortilla, you have yourself a little sunshine on a plate.

Corn tortillas are made with masa harina, a type of corn flour that's been treated with lime-water to soften the corn. This, along with many of the other components in this dish, can be easily prepared in advance for a completely delicious and stress-free breakfast.

Charred salsa Preheat a grill over high heat.

Place tomatoes, onion, and jalapeño on the grill and char for 3 to 5 minutes, turning occasionally, until they are almost completely black. Transfer to a plate.

Remove the stem from the jalapeño. Place the tomatoes, onion, and jalapeño in a blender. Add garlic, cilantro, oil, and salt and pulse for 2 seconds for a chunky salsa (or longer if you prefer it smoother). Set aside.

Refried beans Heat oil in a large frying pan over medium heat. Add onion and sauté for 3 minutes or until softened. Add garlic and mashed beans and cook, stirring constantly with a wooden spoon, for

5 minutes or until cooked through. Season with salt. Keep warm.

Tortillas Put masa harina in a large mixing bowl. Make a well in the center and add lard (or oil), salt, and 1½ cups cold water. Using your hands, knead the mixture for 2 minutes or until it becomes a smooth, uniform, and pliable dough. If necessary, add more cold water, 1 tablespoon at a time. (Do not overmix or tortillas will be tough.)

Divide dough into 8 portions and cover with a damp dish towel. Roll a piece of dough into a ball and place it between two pieces of plastic wrap. Using a rolling pin, flatten the dough as thin as possible. (Alternatively, use a tortilla press to flatten the balls into tortillas.) Repeat with the remaining dough, stacking the tortillas, separated by parchment paper to prevent sticking, as you go. If you make them a day in advance, wrap in plastic wrap and store in the refrigerator.

Heat a large frying pan (or griddle) over high heat. Place a tortilla in the pan and cook for 1 to 1½ minutes, until puffy. Flip over and cook for another minute. Wrap in a dish towel on a plate to keep warm. Repeat until all the tortillas are cooked.

Poached eggs

1 tsp white vinegar

1 tsp salt

8 large eggs

Assembly

½ cup queso fresco, crumbled

½ bunch cilantro, chopped

Poached eggs In a large saucepan, bring 2 quarts water to a boil. Add vinegar and salt, keeping water at a near boil. Crack each egg into a cup and carefully lower, one by one, into the water. (Reduce heat if the water is coming to a boil.) Poach for 3 minutes for a runny yolk. Using a slotted spoon, transfer eggs to a paper towel–lined plate.

Assembly Place 2 tortillas on each plate and spread a thin layer of refried beans on top of each. Top each with a poached egg, then spoon over some salsa. Finish with queso fresco and cilantro. Serve immediately.

Note: Any leftover salsa can be served with tortilla chips as a tasty snack.

3 tsp kosher salt, plus extra to taste (divided)

12 large shrimp, peeled, deveined, and cut into ½-inch pieces

8 oz fresh white fish, cut into ½-inch cubes

8 cherry tomatoes, halved

1 medium cucumber, cut into ½-inch cubes

¼ red onion, finely chopped

1 jalapeño pepper, seeded and finely chopped

1 Tbsp extra-virgin olive oil

Juice of 1 lime

Juice of ½ lemon

2 Tbsp orange juice

Cilantro, for garnish

Store-bought corn nuts or roasted fava beans, for garnish

Lime and lemon wedges, for garnish

Fish and Shrimp Ceviche

SERVES 4 Ceviche in its most basic form is raw fish "cooked" in citrus juices. Here, sweet shrimp and white fish are brightened with lime and lemon juice and balanced with a hint of chile heat and fresh herbs, making this "whip it up and eat" ceviche an instant favorite. The ceviche at Broken Barrel is served with a little nostalgia. "It's how my father makes it," says Hilda Ysusi. "Not too spicy, and with a little crunch."

Bring 4 cups water to a boil in a saucepan and add 2 teaspoons salt. Add shrimp and poach for 1 minute. Meanwhile, fill a large bowl with ice water. Drain shrimp, then transfer to the ice bath and let sit for 3 minutes. Drain.

In a bowl, stir together shrimp, raw fish, tomatoes, cucumber, onion, jalapeño, oil, citrus juices, and remaining 1 teaspoon salt. Gently mix and adjust seasoning as needed. Cover and refrigerate for at least 4 hours.

To serve, spoon ceviche onto a large serving plate and garnish with cilantro, corn nuts (or fava beans), and citrus wedges.

Cacao & Cardamom

ANNIE RUPANI

⭐ Trust a chocolatier to have a porcini chocolate bar in her purse. Whether she's eating or working with it, Annie Rupani always covets good chocolate. "It's true, I'm a total chocoholic."

Rupani, a former law student, had just completed her LSAT in 2011 when she found herself researching chocolate classes. What began as a chocolate hobby grew into a passion as she discovered more about the versatility of chocolate. The next thing she knew, she had enrolled in a ten-day chocolate course in Malaysia. "The world of chocolate is so fascinating and incredibly diverse," she says. Rupani launched Cacao & Cardamom, a fine chocolate confectionery, in 2013. A year later, she opened her first shop and café in the Galleria area and, not too long after, another shop in River Oaks.

The talented chocolatier, with her flair for combining spices, creates little bonbons with eye-popping flavor. Signature creations include ginger ganache and black sesame praline, strawberry fruit paste laced with the floral spice of Sichuan peppercorns, and white chocolate subtly aromatic with cardamom and rosewater. A pyramid-shaped ganache is spiced with ancho and guajillo chiles, while a dark chocolate shell, painted in sunny orange and yellow hues, encases a sweet and fruity mango caramel. Mango reminds Rupani of summers spent in Pakistan. "My mom would bring home a box of mangoes, and we'd squeeze them from the inside out and eat them like a pop," she recalls.

Her hand-painted chocolates are works of art, with exquisitely glossy chocolate shells that "snap" at first bite. At the 2018 International Chocolate Awards, Rupani earned silver for her five-spice praline with milk chocolate and passionfruit ganache. It's a recognition that firmly positions this Houston-based chocolatier among the best in the world.

2 cardamom pods

½ tsp coriander seeds

1 (13.5-oz) can
   coconut milk

1 tsp cocoa powder

1 slice ginger, peeled

½ tsp ground cassia
   or cinnamon

Pinch of salt

2 oz good-quality
   chocolate (preferably
   Valrhona 64% Manjari)

2 oz good-quality dark
   chocolate (preferably
   Valrhona 72% Araguani)

Whipped cream (optional)

Roasted pistachio nibs,
   cardamom pods,
   chocolate callets,
   for garnish (optional)

Spiced Drinking Chocolate

SERVES 2 Dark chocolate, ginger, a hint of cardamom, and cassia come together in this hot chocolate. Either cassia or cinnamon can be used in this recipe (both are tree barks), though chocolatier Annie Rupani prefers cassia. "It is inherently sweeter, more complex, and pungent than cinnamon, so a little goes a long way," she explains. "It also has a high oil content, which contributes to its robust flavor."

Using a mortar and pestle, lightly crack cardamom pods and coriander seeds. In a saucepan, combine coconut milk, cocoa powder, ginger, cardamom, coriander, cassia (or cinnamon), and salt. Bring to a boil, then immediately reduce heat to low and simmer for 20 minutes to steep. Strain and discard the solids.

Return mixture to the saucepan. Add both chocolates and stir over medium heat until chocolates have melted.

Divide between two cups and serve with whipped cream, if using. Garnish with pistachio nibs, cardamom pods, and/or chocolate callets, if using.

3 cups raw cashews

1½ cups granulated sugar

1 Tbsp lemon juice

1½ oz good-quality milk chocolate (preferably Valrhona 40% Jivara)

1 tsp ground cassia or cinnamon

Pinch of Himalayan pink salt

4 oz good-quality couverture chocolate (preferably Valrhona 70% Guanaja) (see Note)

Note: If you use bar chocolate, add 1 to 2 tablespoons shortening or cocoa butter, to make the melted chocolate smoother and easier to work with.

Cashew-Cinnamon Praline Bonbons

MAKES AT LEAST 15 Praline is a wonderfully versatile dessert that can be had on its own, served with coffee in the afternoon, or crumbled over ice cream. In this recipe, chocolatier Annie Rupani shares her technique for making chocolate molds, but you can opt to make truffles instead: Using a large melon baller, scoop mixture to create a sphere. Quickly roll between your hands, dip it in melted chocolate, and set on a wire rack. Dust cinnamon on top and let cool. Repeat until all the mixture is used up.

Preheat oven to 350°F. Line a baking sheet with parchment paper.

Spread cashews on the prepared baking sheet and toast for 7 to 10 minutes, until fragrant and lightly colored. Set aside to cool. Measure out ½ cup cashews, coarsely chop, and reserve for later.

In a medium saucepan, combine sugar, lemon juice, and ¼ cup water. Cook over medium heat for 10 to 12 minutes, untouched, until the caramel is amber in color, bubbly, and sweet smelling (or until a candy thermometer reaches 235°F to 240°F). Brush down the sides of the pan with a damp pastry brush to remove any sugar crystals that have formed.

Pour the caramel directly over the cashews in a thin layer and let cool.

Break up the caramel cashews into smaller pieces, then process in a food processor for 4 to 5 minutes, until the praline is very fine and has a peanut butter–like consistency. Transfer to a bowl.

Put the milk chocolate into a microwave-safe bowl and heat for 30 seconds in the microwave to melt. (Heat for another 15 to 30 seconds, if necessary.) Stir. To the bowl of praline, add the melted chocolate, reserved ½ cup chopped cashews, cassia (or cinnamon), and salt and mix quickly before the chocolate solidifies. Pour into a piping bag and lay flat (tip up) until ready to use. (If making truffles, refrigerate to cool completely.)

Set aside a quarter of the couverture chocolate and break up the rest into a bowl. Microwave in 45-second intervals, stirring with a rubber spatula after each interval, until chocolate is melted and smooth and the temperature has reached 115°F to 120°F. Let sit for 8 minutes.

Add the reserved chocolate to the mixture, a handful at a time, stirring constantly until chocolate crystals form, the mixture thickens, and the temperature drops to 86°F. (This process is known

as seeding.) Once the proper temperature is reached, stop adding the chocolate. Reheat chocolate mixture until the temperature reaches 89°F and you are ready to mold!

Fill a 15-hole chocolate mold with the tempered chocolate. Shake the mold, then tap it on the counter to remove any air bubbles. Be sure the chocolate reaches all the crevices of the mold. Let sit for 30 seconds, then immediately flip the mold over a baking sheet to allow excess chocolate to drip out (reserve leftover chocolate for later). When the drips slow down, turn the mold face up and scrape the surface to tidy the edges of the cavities. Place the mold on parchment paper. (For thinner shells, tap the mold gently all over with a wooden spoon to encourage more chocolate to drip out.) Let sit for 5 minutes or until the shells have set.

To make the bonbons, melt any chocolate leftover from the mold. Fill the shells with praline mixture and pour the melted chocolate overtop to seal. Place the mold in the freezer for 15 minutes.

Remove the bonbons from the mold and serve.

Carol Kay's / Craft Burger

SHANNEN AND STACEY TUNE

Shannen "Tune"

When Shannen Tune opened his food truck in 2016, he earned the moniker of "burger guy" almost immediately. His inventive burgers—thick juicy patties stacked with fanciful toppings and condiments—made the wheeled Craft Burger kitchen one to trail. But there is more to this chef than meets the food-truck eye.

Shannen has twenty years of culinary experience at hotel restaurants across the country, from Miami and New York City to Las Vegas, Los Angeles, and Austin. When he landed in Houston to become the executive chef at Hotel Derek, his eldest was about to start middle school. "He had changed schools as often as I switched hotels, and it was time to settle," Shannen explains. By January 2016, Shannen had left the hotel side of the industry, and he hasn't looked back. It was a good decision all around. First off, he became the first Houston-based chef to win *Chopped* (see the episode "Beg, Borrow or Eel"), wowing the judges with his chicken-fried Cornish hen.

Together with his wife and business partner, Stacey (the two met in culinary school in Miami), he launched Dining with the Tunes (a catering business with cooking classes). The couple's next culinary collaboration is finding a brick-and-mortar in the newly developed Railway Heights food court in 2019. Named after their mothers, Carol Kay's will offer the type of soul food they grew up with. "Stacey, who was raised in Jamaica, makes the best jerk chicken," reveals Shannen.

Craft Burger opened in 2018 as a food-hall restaurant in the upscale downtown Finn Hall, where fans can find delectable burgers like Morning After (the patty stacked with mixed greens, tomato, smoked Gouda, potato hash, candied bacon, and an egg, all held together by two bacon-cheddar waffles) from none other than their favorite "burger guy."

▶ **Fried Chicken with Braised Collards** | p. 51

Thanks for the Love and Support

The Tunes

Brined chicken

½ cup kosher salt

½ cup granulated sugar

Sprig of rosemary

Sprig of thyme

Sprig of sage

½ lemon, halved

½ lime, halved

½ orange, halved

1 (2- to 3-lb) whole chicken

Braised collard greens

1 Tbsp vegetable oil

1 yellow onion, finely chopped

4 cloves garlic, crushed

1 smoked turkey neck

1 Scotch bonnet or habanero pepper

2 sprigs thyme

½ cup apple cider vinegar

½ cup maple syrup

6 cups chicken stock or water

3 bunches collard greens, leaves stripped and chopped

Salt and black pepper

Fried chicken

6 cups vegetable oil

1 Brined Chicken (see here)

2 large eggs

2 cups buttermilk

¼ cup hot sauce

2 cups all-purpose flour (divided)

2 Tbsp kosher salt

2 Tbsp black pepper

1 Tbsp garlic salt

1 Tbsp onion powder

2 cloves garlic, crushed

2 sprigs thyme

Fried Chicken with Braised Collards

SERVES 4 TO 5 This is soul food at its best: hearty, satisfying, and loaded with flavor. This recipe delivers irresistibly crisp fried chicken with a crunchy bite and juicy, tender meat. And then we have the collard greens—smoky, sweet, and with a pleasant heat.

Brined chicken Bring 2 quarts of water to boil in a stockpot. Add salt, sugar, rosemary, thyme, and sage and boil for 5 minutes. Set aside to cool.

Add the lemon, lime, and orange and carefully lower in the chicken, making sure it's fully submerged. Cover the pot and refrigerate for 4 to 6 hours.

Rinse brine off chicken and pat dry with paper towel.

Braised collards Heat oil in a heavy-bottomed stockpot over medium heat. Add onion, garlic, and turkey neck and sauté for 10 minutes. Add Scotch bonnet (or habanero), thyme, vinegar, syrup, and stock (or water). Bring to a boil and simmer for 1 hour.

Add collard greens, reduce heat to low, and braise gently for 40 to 50 minutes, until greens are tender. Discard turkey neck and habanero. Season greens with salt and pepper, and keep warm.

Fried chicken Heat oil in a deep fryer or deep saucepan to a temperature of 325°F.

Portion chicken into 10 pieces (2 drumsticks, 2 thighs, 2 wings, and 2 breasts, each breast halved widthwise).

In a medium bowl, whisk eggs for 1 minute or until foamy. Pour in buttermilk and hot sauce and whisk for another 30 seconds.

Add ½ cup flour to a shallow bowl, then pour the egg mixture into another. In a third bowl, combine the remaining 1½ cups flour, salt, pepper, garlic salt, and onion powder. Season to taste.

Dredge a piece of chicken in the plain flour, roll it in the egg mixture, then coat it in the seasoned flour. (Use one hand for the dry steps and another for the wet step.) Transfer to a plate and repeat with the remaining chicken.

Carefully add garlic and thyme to the hot oil. Working in batches, if necessary, to avoid overcrowding, gently lower chicken into the oil and deep-fry for 12 minutes or until golden crisp. Using a slotted spoon, transfer to a paper towel–lined plate and let cool for 5 minutes.

Serve immediately with the collard greens.

Jamaican oxtail

2 to 3 lbs oxtail

2 Tbsp olive oil (divided)

3 cloves garlic, chopped

1 small onion, chopped

1 tsp onion powder

1 tsp garlic powder

1 tsp salt

1 tsp black pepper

5 allspice berries

1 Scotch bonnet or habanero pepper

1 tsp chopped thyme

2 scallions, chopped

Rice and peas

½ cup dried pigeon peas or red beans, soaked overnight

1 clove garlic, finely chopped

2 scallions, chopped

1 tsp chopped thyme

1 tsp salt

1 cup coconut milk

2 cups medium-grain rice

1 Tbsp butter

Jamaican Oxtail Arancini

MAKES 12 ARANCINI Jamaican oxtail arancini are a special treat at Carol Kay's: tender, melt-in-the-mouth oxtail is encased in rice, then lightly breaded and fried. Rice and peas are traditionally prepared with plump pigeon peas, which are widely available throughout the Caribbean, but are equally excellent with red beans. Leftover rice and peas make a delicious next meal with the oxtail and its braising jus.

Jamaican oxtail In a large bowl, mix oxtail with 1 tablespoon oil, garlic, onion, onion and garlic powders, salt, and black pepper. Cover and refrigerate overnight to marinate.

Heat the remaining 1 tablespoon olive oil in a large saucepan over high heat. Wipe the oxtails clean with kitchen paper. Sear oxtail for 2 minutes on each side, then transfer to a plate. Deglaze the pan with 2 cups water. Add the onions and garlic from the oxtail marinade, along with the allspice, Scotch bonnet (or habanero), and thyme. Return the oxtail to the pan and bring to a boil. Cover, reduce heat to low, and simmer for 4 to 6 hours, until tender.

Add scallions and simmer for 5 to 6 minutes. Remove from heat and let cool to room temperature. Remove the oxtail from the bones. Discard the bones. Reserve the braising liquid.

Rice and peas Rinse the soaked peas (or red beans). Put peas, garlic, and 2 cups water into a large saucepan and cook for 1 to 2 hours on low heat, until peas are tender.

Add scallions, thyme, salt, and coconut milk. Bring to a boil, then add rice and butter. Return to the boil, reduce heat to medium-low, and cover. Cook for 30 to 35 minutes, until rice is tender.

Arancini

2 cups Rice and Peas
  (see here)

½ cup reserved oxtail
  braising liquid
  (see Oxtail recipe)

¼ cup grated Parmesan

1 cup Jamaican Oxtail
  (see here)

1 cup all-purpose flour

2 large eggs, beaten

1½ cups panko
  breadcrumbs

4 cups peanut oil

Arancini In a frying pan, combine the rice and peas and reserved oxtail braising liquid and bring to a boil over medium-high heat. Stir continuously for 3 to 5 minutes, until the rice mixture has a porridge-like consistency. Spread out on a baking sheet to cool.

In a large bowl, combine the cooled rice mixture and Parmesan.

Using a ½-cup measuring cup, scoop enough rice mixture to create a ball that fits comfortably in your palm (about 2 inches diameter). Shape into a patty, put about a tablespoon of oxtail in the center, and shape the rice back around into a tight ball. Repeat with the remaining rice mixture and oxtail.

Place flour, eggs, and breadcrumbs in separate shallow bowls. Dredge an arancini in the flour, then in egg and finally in breadcrumbs. Repeat with the remaining arancini. Cover with paper towel and refrigerate until needed.

Heat oil in a saucepan over high heat. (The oil should be deep enough to cover arancini during frying.) Drop a breadcrumb into the oil; if it sizzles, the oil is hot enough. Working in batches to avoid overcrowding, carefully lower arancini into the pan and cook for 6 minutes or until golden. Using a slotted spoon, transfer arancini to a paper towel–lined plate. Serve immediately.

Cherry Block Craft Butcher & Seasonal Kitchen

FELIX FLOREZ AND JESSICA DESHAM TIMMONS

★ When two locally focused minds think alike, great things happen. As co-chefs and co-owners, Felix Florez and Jessica DeSham Timmons opened Cherry Block Craft Butcher & Seasonal Kitchen, a home-grown steakhouse in Bravery Chef Hall in 2019.

If there is anyone in the Houston food industry who knows his meat, it's rancher, pit master, butcher, and chef Florez. With a big heart for conservation and sustain-ability, Florez (who also happens to be an accomplished sommelier) founded Black Hill Ranch to supply Houston restaurants with humanely raised meat. He began raising heritage-breed hogs and soon expanded to cattle and lamb.

Chef DeSham Timmons brings to the business a wealth of restaurant experi-ence from her years at Landry's and then the Redneck Country Club. As one of the founding members of Foodways Texas, a nonprofit committed to preserving and recording Texas's rich culinary history, DeSham Timmons is driven by local gastronomy. Her philosophy is simple: "When you have the best-quality ingredients, they speak for themselves."

Being a counter restaurant in Bravery Hall allows for a somewhat whimsical approach to the steakhouse concept. Small plates like whipped lardo and bread, shrimp and cracklins, charcuterie, and mushroom toast shine alongside house-butchered cuts of pork, beef, and lamb. To interact with the chef, simply dine at the counter, in front of the wood-fired grill—it's her face you'll see most when you sit there.

Sharing the same vision, Florez and DeSham Timmons built the menu together, taking a seasonal approach and based on their inherent love for authentic Southern foods. They're responsible ranchers who ensure that all the meat at Cherry Block comes from Black Hill Ranch or other Texas farms. Florez says it best: "We are Texans feeding Texans."

▶ **Seared Pork Chops with Strawberry-Sorghum Glaze and Boudin Mashed Potatoes** | p. 58–59

Menudo bites

2 cups dried hominy (whole kernel)	1 Tbsp dried Mexican oregano
4 cups chicken stock	1 tsp black peppercorns
2 poblano peppers	2 dried ancho chiles, stemmed and seeded
3 lbs clean honeycomb beef tripe	¼ cup (½ stick) butter
3 smoked pork trotters	½ cup heavy cream
5 cloves garlic	1 yard egg, lightly beaten
1 large red onion, chopped	Salt and black pepper
	Pico de Gallo (see here)

Menudo Bites

MAKES 10 CAKES Rancher-chef Felix Florez can make something delicious from any cut or part of an animal. Here, he elevates honeycomb tripe in a reimagined *menudo*, the classic Mexican beef tripe soup: crisp-fried hominy cakes are capped with pan-fried flakes of tripe, all richly soaked with the stewed flavors of roasted peppers, aromatic herbs, and smoky trotters. Goya-branded dried hominy and Mexican oregano (which has distinct citrusy notes) can be found at Fiesta supermarkets.

Menudo bites Soak hominy in a bowl of water for 12 to 24 hours. Drain, then transfer to a saucepan.

Add just enough water to cover the hominy. Pour in stock and bring to a boil. Reduce heat to low, cover, and simmer for 2 hours. Add more hot water as needed to keep the hominy covered.

Meanwhile, preheat a grill over high heat. Grill poblano peppers for 5 minutes or until softened, blistered, and charred all over. Transfer peppers to a plastic bag and let sit for 10 minutes to loosen the skin. When cool enough to handle, remove skins, stems, and seeds (do not rinse under the tap). Coarsely chop.

Drain hominy and transfer to a large stockpot. Add tripe, trotters, garlic, onion, oregano, and peppercorns. Add enough water to cover ingredients by 4 inches and bring to a boil. Reduce heat to low, cover, and simmer for 2 hours. Add chiles, then simmer for another hour.

Strain mixture into a large colander set over a large bowl. Separate tripe from the hominy and set aside. Pour the liquid into a saucepan and add trotters. Simmer on low, uncovered, until liquid is reduced by half and sauce is thick enough to coat the back of a spoon. Strain menudo sauce into another saucepan and keep warm. Transfer trotters to a cutting board and let cool. Pick off the meat and finely chop. Discard bones.

In a large bowl, combine the well-drained hominy, trotters meat, butter, cream, and egg. Using a potato masher or immersion blender, mash the hominy mixture until it is the consistency of thick, creamy polenta. Season with salt and pepper.

Line a baking sheet with parchment paper. Spread mixture on top of the prepared baking sheet to a 1-inch thickness. Refrigerate, uncovered, until chilled and set.

Pico de gallo

2 large ripe tomatoes, chopped

1 red onion, chopped

1 jalapeño pepper, seeded and chopped

2 Tbsp chopped cilantro

Juice of 1 lime

Pinch of salt

Assembly

Cornstarch, for dusting

2 Tbsp canola oil

Pico de gallo Stir together tomatoes, onion, jalapeño, and cilantro. Add lime juice and salt and gently toss with a spoon. Cover and refrigerate until needed.

Assembly Cut the chilled hominy mixture into 3- × 5-inch rectangles. Lightly dust cornstarch over the hominy cakes (it will help crisp them).

Cut the tripe into 2- x 2-inch pieces. Heat oil in a frying pan over medium-high heat. Add tripe and fry for 1 to 1½ minutes on each side, until crisp. Transfer to a plate and set aside.

In the same frying pan set over high heat, add hominy cakes and pan-fry for 1 minute on each side or until crisp. Keep warm.

To serve family-style, spoon warm menudo sauce onto a serving platter. Place the hominy cakes in the sauce, and top with the pan-fried tripe. Garnish with a tablespoon of pico de gallo and serve immediately.

Boudin mashed potatoes

1 (¾-lb) link butcher-made boudin, casing removed

8 Yukon Gold potatoes, peeled and quartered

½ cup (1 stick) butter, room temperature

⅓ cup whole milk, room temperature

½ Tbsp salt

1 tsp black pepper

Strawberry-sorghum glaze

½ cup fruity vinegar (preferably sugar cane vinegar)

2 Tbsp sorghum syrup or molasses (see Note)

1 Tbsp puréed strawberries

1 tsp salt

1 tsp hot sauce (preferably Crystal)

½ tsp black pepper

1 Tbsp butter, cold

Note: Sorghum syrup, extracted from the green juice of sorghum grass, is a traditional Southern product with a mild molasses flavor that is used here to lift the glaze. It can be purchased at Central Market, or on Amazon.

Seared Pork Chops with Strawberry-Sorghum Glaze and Boudin Mashed Potatoes

SERVES 4 When you fill your kitchen with the aromas of caramelizing chops, you won't need to call anyone to the table! Between the boudin-stippled mash and the sweet-tart glaze, this recipe captures the great flavors of Texas in honest food that doesn't take a whole lot of time to prepare—though we recommend preparing the collards a day in advance to develop the flavors.

Boudin mashed potatoes Fry boudin meat in a frying pan over medium-high heat for 2 to 3 minutes, until slightly crispy and brown. Set aside.

Put potatoes in a saucepan of water and bring to a boil. Cook for 10 to 12 minutes, until tender. Drain and return to the pan. Add butter, milk, salt, and pepper and mash until smooth. Stir in three-quarters of the boudin and reserve the rest for garnish.

Strawberry-sorghum glaze Put all ingredients except butter into a saucepan and cook over medium heat for 5 minutes or until mixture is reduced by half and thick enough to coat the back of a spoon. Remove from heat and stir in butter until it's melted.

Braised collards Heat lard in a large saucepan over medium-high heat. Add onion, garlic, tasso, and pepper and sauté for 3 to 5 minutes, until onion is browned. Add collard greens and stir to coat.

Pour in enough stock to cover the greens. Bring to a boil, then reduce heat to medium and simmer for 45 minutes, stirring frequently. Add vinegar, hot sauce, and salt and simmer for another 15 minutes.

Braised collards

- 1 Tbsp lard
- 1 large yellow onion, finely chopped
- 4 cloves garlic, finely chopped
- 1 cup tasso, cut into ¼-inch dice (see Note)
- ½ Tbsp black pepper
- 2 bunches collard greens, cleaned, stems trimmed, and leaves cut into 4-inch pieces
- 2 qts chicken stock
- 1 Tbsp fruity vinegar (preferably sugar cane vinegar)
- 1 tsp Crystal hot sauce
- ½ Tbsp kosher salt

Pork chops

- 4 bone-in heritage-breed pork chops
- Kosher salt and black pepper
- 1 to 2 Tbsp lard
- Strawberry-Sorghum Glaze (see here)
- Chopped parsley, for garnish

Pork chops Preheat oven to 350°F.

Generously season pork chops with salt and pepper. Heat lard in a cast-iron pan over high heat until almost smoking. Add chops and sear for 2 minutes on each side or until golden brown. Spoon enough glaze over each chop to coat, then put the pan in the oven and roast for 10 to 12 minutes, until pork is cooked through. Remove from oven and let rest for 5 minutes.

Transfer chops to four serving plates and spoon more glaze overtop. Serve with boudin mash potatoes and braised collards, and garnished with the reserved boudin and chopped parsley.

Note: A Cajun delicacy, tasso is smoked, seasoned pork that's often sold as ham, though it's actually from the fattier shoulder cut, rather than the leg. Rarely eaten on its own, this flavoring ingredient adds a peppery kick to beans, meat stews, and rice dishes such as jambalaya. It can be replaced with spicy chorizo or Canadian bacon, but the flavor will be slightly different.

Common Bond Café & Bakery

MATT BAUM

★ Walk into Common Bond on any given morning and you'll be arrested by the smell of fresh-baked bread, mingling with the aroma of caramel, cinnamon, and freshly roasted coffee. Breakfast—even something as simple as a plain croissant and coffee—has always been a scrumptious affair here. Common Bond is a bakery, cake shop, and café all at once.

If you can pry yourself away from the tempting showcase of chocolate-dipped eclairs, turtle brownies, fresh fruit pies, and tartlets of all flavors, you'll find a full menu boasting an array of tasty salads, sandwiches such as a Paris-meets-Houston Croque Madame (grilled ham and cheese with jalapeño béchamel), and specialties like duck confit braised with white beans, pork belly, and sausage—you know, just to keep things interesting.

The menu swings happily between Gulf Coast favorites (think blackened shrimp with Creole sauce and grits) and classic French fare (think slow-braised beef Bourguignon), compliments of executive chef Matt Baum. Trained in classic French cuisine at Le Cordon Bleu in Austin, Baum brings an intriguing culinary mix to the table. Born and raised in Houston, Baum says it was his Filipino grandmother who inspired the cook in him: "My grandmother taught me that good food can't be rushed." Good food is also worth the wait: five years after the bakery and café first opened, Common Bond expands to a second location in the Heights, with three more locations in the works.

▶ **Sweet Corn Bisque with Crabmeat and Crispy Bacon** | p. 62
with Crispy Sprouts | p. 63

Corn bisque

1 Tbsp butter

1 large yellow onion, chopped

4 cups frozen sweet corn

¼ cup dry sherry

2 cups heavy cream

1 cup whole milk

½ Tbsp kosher salt, or to taste

Pinch of ground white pepper, plus extra to taste

Pinch of onion powder

Juice of ½ lemon

Assembly

½ to 1 cup bacon, chopped

½ to 1 cup jumbo lump crabmeat

¼ cup extra-virgin olive oil

1 Tbsp chopped chives

Sweet Corn Bisque with Crabmeat and Crispy Bacon

SERVES 4 The sweetness from the corn in this soup is perfectly countered by the saltiness of crispy bacon, savory-sweet crabmeat, and refreshing chives, all of which add the perfect amount of decadence. The recipe requires you to press the soup through a fine-mesh sieve, and though that might seem fussy, the resulting velvety texture elevates the soup to fine-dining quality.

Corn bisque Melt butter in a large saucepan over medium heat. Add onion and sauté for 8 to 10 minutes, until softened and caramelized. Stir in corn and increase heat to medium-high. Carefully add sherry (it may cause steam) and cook for 1 minute or until reduced by half.

Pour in cream and milk and add salt, pepper, and onion powder. Bring to a gentle boil, then reduce heat to medium-low and simmer gently for 15 minutes to infuse flavors.

Using an immersion blender, purée until smooth. Add lemon juice and adjust seasoning to taste. Strain soup through a fine-mesh strainer.

Assembly Heat a small nonstick frying pan over high heat. Sauté bacon for 2 minutes or until crisp and golden. Transfer to a paper towel–lined plate to drain and set aside.

Ladle bisque into individual bowls. Garnish with crispy bacon and crabmeat, then drizzle oil overtop and finish with a sprinkle of chopped chives. Serve immediately.

Caramelized onions

1 Tbsp canola oil

1 red onion, thinly sliced

¼ cup packed light brown sugar

1 Tbsp balsamic vinegar

1 tsp black pepper

½ tsp salt

Brussels sprouts

Vegetable oil, for deep-frying

4 cups Brussels sprouts, halved

1 Tbsp olive oil

¼ cup diced pancetta

½ cup Caramelized Onions (see here)

1 tsp kosher salt

Salt and black pepper

1 Tbsp honey

Crispy Sprouts

SERVES 5 TO 6 When at Common Bond, it's tempting to choose something that's been baked at this artisanal bakery, but don't overlook a simple side, such as crispy sprouts. The Brussels sprouts—tossed with caramelized onion, crispy pancetta, and a touch of honey—make for an excellent side or snack. And now you can make them at home. Use medium to large sprouts, which will crisp up nicely and soften to the core.

Caramelized onions Heat oil in a large frying pan over medium heat. Add onion and sauté for 10 minutes or until softened and beginning to caramelize. Stir in sugar, vinegar, pepper, and salt and cook for another 10 minutes or until syrupy.

Remove from heat and let cool. (Any leftovers can be stored in an airtight container in the refrigerator for up to 1 week—these onions are a great addition to a roast beef sandwich.)

Brussels sprouts Heat vegetable oil in a deep fryer or deep saucepan to a temperature of 350°F. Carefully lower Brussels sprouts into the oil and deep-fry for 2 minutes or until crisp on the outside and a little hard still on the inside (the sprouts will cook some more when tossed with the caramelized onions). Using a slotted spoon, transfer Brussels sprouts to a paper towel–lined bowl to drain.

Heat olive oil in a large frying pan over high heat. Add pancetta and fry for 1 minute or until crisp. Reduce heat to medium-high, add Brussels sprouts and sauté for 2 minutes. Add caramelized onions and toss for 1 to 2 minutes. Season with salt and pepper.

Transfer to a serving bowl, drizzle honey over the top, and serve immediately.

Dessert Gallery & Café

SARA BROOK

⭐ You *can* have your cake and eat it too. But at Dessert Gallery Bakery & Café, it's a surprisingly difficult task when all the confections on display are so irresistible. You might go for a slice of white chocolate cheesecake adorned with fresh berries; a piece of chocolate cake with layers of meringue, mousse, brownies, and ganache; or a happy confetti-colored unicorn cupcake. There are also cookies and cake pops galore to choose from.

Owner Sara Brook has poured her passion into baking. Back in 1983, fresh out of college, she operated her first dessert business out of her parents' kitchen. In 1995, after running several dessert businesses, she opened Dessert Gallery Bakery & Café, where she continues to be supported by a strong team, whom she lovingly refers to as her "DG family." (Some of her staff have been with her from day one, and a few of their kids now work there too.)

The pastry chef is at home in her commissary, just a few miles south of the café. This is where the sweet magic happens: chocolate frosting is made for her popular old-fashioned diner cake, pastry leaves are draped over double-crust apple pies, and French macarons are filled with Swiss buttercream or chocolate ganache. Her most popular celebration cake is Jennifer's Birthday Cake, a fudgy, dark chocolate cake brightened with colorful sprinkles that's named after her daughter, who turned five the week after the shop opened. Brook's handcrafted cookies, cakes, and desserts come with a little nostalgia and a lot of love, reminding us of the fresh-baked cakes of our childhood.

▶ **Luscious Lemon Squares** | p. 66
and Pecan Pie Bars | p. 67

2¼ cups all-purpose flour (divided)

1 cup (2 sticks) butter, cut into ½-inch cubes, plus extra for greasing

½ cup confectioners' sugar, plus extra for dusting

4 large eggs

2 cups granulated sugar

⅓ cup lemon juice

½ tsp baking powder

Luscious Lemon Squares

MAKES 12 (3-INCH) SQUARES These fuss-free bars, with their creamy and tart lemon curd baked on top of a sweet crumb base, make for a favorite morning treat with coffee or potluck dessert. There is one thing key to the delicious-ness of lemon squares: use fresh lemon juice.

Preheat oven to 350°F. Grease a 9- × 13-inch baking pan.

Place 2 cups flour, butter, and confectioners' sugar in a large mixing bowl. Using a hand mixer, mix together for 4 to 5 minutes, until mixture is smooth. Press mixture into the prepared pan. Bake for 20 to 25 minutes, until cooked and lightly colored.

In a large mixing bowl, whisk together eggs, sugar, and lemon juice for 2 to 3 minutes, until well combined. (Or use a handheld mixer.)

Using a spatula, fold in the remaining ¼ cup flour and baking powder for 1 minute or until fully incorporated. Pour filling over the baked crust and bake for 25 minutes or until filling is set. Let cool before cutting into 12 squares.

Dust with confectioners' sugar and serve.

Crust

2 cups all-purpose flour

1 cup (2 sticks) butter, softened, plus extra for greasing

½ cup granulated sugar

1 egg white, beaten

Filling

2 cups + 2 Tbsp brown sugar

¼ cup all-purpose flour

¾ tsp fine salt

3 Tbsp maple syrup

¼ cup (½ stick) butter, melted

4 large eggs

2¼ cups chopped pecans

Pecan Pie Bars

MAKES 12 BARS This classic, crowd-pleasing dessert is perfect for gatherings. In its simplest form, we have a rich caramel-pecan topping on a buttery crumb base, but if you're looking for an elegant presentation, follow Sara Brook's advice and cut the bars in various shapes: diamonds, triangles, circles—as you like—for an appealing assortment on the dessert tray. In Houston, the best pecans are to be found in late fall, when they come straight from the groves to the local farmers' markets.

Crust Preheat oven to 350°F. Grease a 9- × 13-inch baking pan.

Place flour, butter, and sugar in a large mixing bowl. Using a hand mixer, mix together for 4 to 5 minutes, until mixture is smooth.

Press mixture evenly into the bottom of the prepared pan. Using a fork, prick dough, then brush the surface with egg white. Bake for 25 to 30 minutes, until lightly golden.

Filling In a medium bowl, combine sugar, flour, and salt. Whisk in maple syrup, butter, and eggs for 2 minutes or until well blended. Stir in pecans. Spread topping evenly over the baked crust. Bake for 25 minutes or until golden and filling is set. Let cool before cutting into 12 bars.

Doris Metropolitan

SASH KURGAN AND MICHAL MICHAELI

★ Houston has its share of excellent steakhouses. And then there's Doris Metropolitan. Modern with a chic Levantine ambiance, it's at once breezy and flamboyant. Sit at the central bar and take in a sweeping view, from the bustling open kitchen to the ornate glass-walled meat room housing its dry-aging beef. But it's that this steakhouse is rooted in Middle Eastern cuisine that makes it a standout. The kitchen's stock ingredients include olive oil and lemon juice, preserved lemons, cured olives, labneh (yogurt cheese), and schug, an herb-based hot sauce. And vegetables—cucumbers, cauliflower, artichokes, eggplant, vine-ripened tomatoes—are also essentials.

"We bring a different angle to a steakhouse," says Itai Ben Eli, one of four partners. The concept originated with Doris Butchers, the partners' original artisan butcher shop in Tel Aviv. Upon selling the shop in 2008, they wanted to launch a chef-driven steakhouse that balanced the heaviness of meat with lighter flavors. "And for us Israelis, that means lots of vegetables," explains executive chef Sash Kurgan.

Attention to detail is everywhere—for instance, the complimentary bread service: pastry chef Michal Michaeli's fresh-baked specialty breads are stuffed with smoked eggplant or caramelized onions and feta. If you think the breads are irresistible, just wait for dessert. Michaeli's multidimensional creations speak the same language as the kitchen, as seen in her labneh brûlée hinted with cardamom and white chocolate, and thyme-infused panna cotta draped in raspberry sheets, with rosewater coulis.

Meat mavens will rave about the Butcher Board, a lavish display of various cuts of steak, along with roasted bone marrow. But its ability to satisfy veggie-forward palates with dishes such as roasted cauliflower with tahini and pearl onions, and grilled fresh artichoke nestled in tzatziki, is the reason this steakhouse is in a league of its own.

▶ **Jerusalem Cauliflower Salad** | p. 70-71

Cauliflower

⅓ cup olive oil

1 Tbsp ground paprika

1 tsp salt, plus extra to taste

½ tsp ground turmeric

¼ tsp black pepper

1 cauliflower, cut into bite-size florets

Chickpeas

¼ cup cooked chickpeas, drained

1 Tbsp extra-virgin olive oil

Juice of ½ lemon

¼ tsp salt

¼ tsp ground cumin

¼ tsp black pepper

Schug

2 jalapeño peppers, seeded and roughly chopped

1 clove garlic

2 Tbsp finely chopped cilantro

2 Tbsp finely chopped Italian parsley

1 Tbsp white wine vinegar

1 Tbsp extra-virgin olive oil

Pinch of ground cumin

Salt

Pearl onions

6 pearl onions, peeled and halved

1 Tbsp olive oil

½ tsp salt

Pinch of black pepper

Sprig of thyme

Herb tahini

½ cup tahini

½ bunch Italian parsley

½ bunch cilantro

1 clove garlic, crushed

Juice of ½ lemon

Salt

Jerusalem Cauliflower Salad

SERVES 4 You'll never look at cauliflower the same way again once you've tasted this elegant salad, with its symphony of flavors. The recipe calls for schug, a spicy Yemeni sauce of green chiles and fresh herbs. The sauce keeps in the refrigerator at least 1 week and can be used on anything, from scrambled eggs to grilled steak.

Cauliflower Preheat oven to 350°F. Line a baking sheet with parchment paper.

In a large mixing bowl, combine oil, paprika, salt, turmeric, and pepper. Add cauliflower and toss to coat. Transfer cauliflower to the prepared baking sheet and bake for 20 to 25 minutes, until golden and tender.

Chickpeas Put chickpeas into a bowl. Season with oil, lemon juice, salt, cumin, and pepper, adjusting seasoning to taste. Set aside.

Schug Place all ingredients in a large bowl. Using an immersion blender, pulse for 1 minute or until coarsely mixed. Set aside.

Pearl onions Preheat oven to 350°F. Line a baking sheet with parchment paper.

Place onions, cut-side up, on the prepared baking sheet. Drizzle oil over onions and sprinkle salt and pepper on top. Place thyme in between. Bake for 25 minutes or until onions are golden.

Herb tahini In a food processor, combine tahini and ½ cup cold water. Add parsley, cilantro, and garlic and process until smooth. Add lemon juice, season with salt, and blend for 1 minute, adding more water as needed. The tahini sauce should be thick but still pourable.

Salsa

1 large ripe tomato

½ clove garlic

1 Tbsp extra-virgin olive oil

Salt and black pepper

Assembly

1 cup Herb Tahini (see here)

Chickpeas (see here)

Roasted Pearl Onions (see here)

⅓ cup Schug (see here)

¼ cup Salsa (see here)

1 Tbsp sour cream

1 Tbsp extra-virgin olive oil

Italian parsley, for garnish

1 Tbsp pine nuts

Flaky sea salt

Salsa In a food processor, process all ingredients until mixture is smooth. Refrigerate until needed.

Assembly Smear herb tahini on the bottom of a large serving platter. Place cauliflower florets on top, then scatter chickpeas and pearl onions in between. Spoon schug, salsa, and sour cream between florets. Drizzle oil over top and garnish with parsley. Scatter with pine nuts and finish with a sprinkle of salt.

Pecan crumble

1 cup almond flour

¾ cup (10 Tbsp) all-purpose flour

½ cup packed brown sugar

1 cup chopped pecans

½ cup (1 stick) butter, cut into 1-inch cubes, chilled

Date mousse

1 cup date paste

5 Tbsp whole milk

1 sheet gelatin (4 g), soaked, or 1 tsp gelatin powder

¼ cup heavy whipping cream

1 large egg white

1½ Tbsp granulated sugar

Note: You can find date paste at Phoenicia Specialty Foods. Or make your own by puréeing pitted dates (about 2 cups whole dates will make 1 cup date paste).

White Chocolate–Glazed Date Mousse and Pecan Crumble with Chocolate Sauce

SERVES 4 TO 6 Surprise your dinner guests with a stunning, layered dessert of ultra-smooth date mousse perched on pecan crumble, blanketed with a white chocolate glaze and finished with a luscious dark-chocolate sauce. And as if that weren't enough, both the date mousse and pecan crumble can be made up to 3 days in advance. At the restaurant, the dessert is assembled in individual ring molds lined with acetate, but you can use a loaf pan (or cake mold).

Pecan crumble Preheat oven to 350°F. Line a baking sheet with parchment paper.

Put both flours, sugar, and pecans into a medium bowl. Using your hands, work in the butter for 2 minutes or until clumps form. (Do not overmix.) Spread the mixture onto the prepared baking sheet. Bake for 10 to 12 minutes, until golden brown. Set aside to cool.

Line a 2-lb loaf pan with plastic wrap (with extra wrap for overhang). Press the crumble into the bottom of the loaf pan to achieve a ½-inch depth. (Unbaked crumble can be stored in an airtight container in the freezer for up to 2 months.)

Date mousse In a small saucepan set over medium heat, stir together date paste and milk to form a loose paste. Remove from heat. Whisk in gelatin until dissolved. Set aside to cool.

Meanwhile, in a separate bowl, whip cream to medium-stiff peaks. Fold cream into the cooled date mixture.

In a separate bowl, whip egg white until it has some volume. Gradually add sugar, whipping until a meringue is formed. Fold mixture into date batter. Carefully spread date batter on top of the pecan crumble in the loaf pan, cover with plastic wrap, and freeze until solid, at least 2 hours or overnight.

White chocolate glaze

²/₃ cup (4 oz) good-quality white chocolate, broken into small pieces

3 Tbsp cocoa butter or butter

¾ sheet gelatin (3 g), soaked, or ¾ tsp gelatin powder

½ cup heavy whipping cream

1 Tbsp light corn syrup

Chocolate sauce

¼ cup whole milk

3 Tbsp heavy cream

2 Tbsp granulated sugar

²/₃ cup chopped good-quality dark chocolate

White chocolate glaze In a bowl, combine chocolate, butter, and gelatin. Set aside.

In a small saucepan, combine cream and corn syrup and bring to a boil. Whisk in chocolate mixture and stir until smooth. Set aside until cooled to 90°F to 93°F or until mixture is the consistency of runny honey.

Assembly Remove the mousse from the freezer. Holding the edges of the plastic wrap, carefully lift it out of the pan. Carefully remove the plastic wrap and transfer to a baking sheet.

Drizzle white chocolate glaze on top until the mousse is completely coated. It should have a mirror glaze, so avoid touching it. If the sides remain a little bare, use an icing spatula (or a butter knife or spreader) to spread the glaze carefully over the sides. Let the glaze set for 10 minutes, then refrigerate until ready to serve.

Chocolate sauce In a small saucepan, combine milk, cream, and sugar and bring to boil.

Put chocolate into a bowl and pour in the hot mixture. Whisk until chocolate is dissolved and sauce is smooth.

Plating Slice the mousse into portions. Arrange on individual plates and drizzle the warm chocolate sauce around it. Serve immediately.

The Dunlavy

JANE WILD

⭐ The Dunlavy has to be one of the most stunning venues in all of Houston. The strikingly beautiful glass house exudes vintage charm with its thirty-nine chandeliers suspended from the ceiling, while three walls of floor-to-ceiling windows transform the outdoor scenery of Buffalo Bayou Park into a live landscape painting.

When Jane Wild became the executive chef for Clark Cooper Concepts' The Dunlavy in spring 2018, she brought great energy to the kitchen. She amped up the menu by giving it a focus on seasonality, sought partnerships with local growers and community gardens, and consolidated a terrific kitchen team. Within months, Wild and her team participated in exciting culinary collaborations with I'll Have What She's Having (a nonprofit raising awareness of women's health) and the annual Butcher's Ball (a fundraiser for local farms and ranches).

Wild loves her team. "Everyone brings their own culinary flavor to the mix," she says. From za'atar nectarine tartine to heirloom tomato shakshouka to homemade tortillas with hibiscus mole, duck, and cactus salad, these recipes make every day at The Dunlavy unique.

Stroll in on any given morning and you'll find a delectable selection of fresh, wholesome fare prepared by the team. Favorites include the baker's board (house pastries, local cheese, and fruit), seasonal grain bowls, and sandwiches made with fresh-baked artisanal bread.

By night, in the light of the shimmering chandeliers, the glass house is at its magical best and usually reserved for private dining events. That's when Wild and team lavish guests with a multicourse feast. Once in a while, though, on a free night, she'll offer a pop-up dinner, which is not to be missed!

Harissa

3 red bell peppers

1 habanero pepper, stemmed and seeded

3 cloves garlic

Bunch of cilantro

2 tsp ground cumin

2 tsp chili flakes

1½ tsp caraway seeds

1 tsp black pepper

¼ tsp salt

Side salad

2 handfuls chopped kale

1 small golden beet, peeled and thinly shaved

½ small fennel bulb, thinly shaved

1 small carrot, shaved into thin ribbons

Juice of 1 small lemon

Sea salt and black pepper

Tartine

4 slices sourdough bread, toasted

¼ cup Harissa (see here)

1 ripe avocado

Juice of ½ lemon

Sea salt and black pepper

Pinch of ground cumin

Pinch of chili flakes

¼ cup cilantro leaves

Sliced boiled egg, crumbled feta, or microgreens (optional)

Salad, to serve

Avocado-Harissa Tartine

SERVES 2 TO 4 The tartine, essentially an open-faced sandwich, is an ever-changing item at The Dunlavy that's led by seasonal ingredients. This version is an indulgent combination of creamy avocado and homemade harissa, and one that you'll make over and over again. Harissa is wonderful in chili, couscous salad, or tomato sauce, or on grilled fish.

Harissa Preheat oven to 400°F.

Place bell peppers on a baking sheet and roast for 20 to 30 minutes, until charred and blistered. Transfer peppers to a plastic bag and let sit for 10 minutes to loosen the skin. When cool enough to handle, remove skin, stem, and seeds (do not rinse under the tap).

In a blender or food processor, blend all ingredients to form a paste. Adjust seasoning to taste. Set aside. (Any leftover harissa can be stored in an airtight container for up to 5 days.)

Side salad In a bowl, add kale, beet, fennel, and carrot. Season with lemon juice, salt, and pepper.

Tartine Spread some harissa paste on each slice of toasted bread.

Cut avocado in half, remove the pit, and scoop halves out of the peel. Cut each into ¼-inch-thick slices, then fan out avocado on top of harissa.

Squeeze lemon juice on top and season with salt and pepper, cumin, and chili flakes. Sprinkle with cilantro and top with sliced egg, feta, or microgreens, if using. Serve with the side salad.

Pie crust

- 2 cups all-purpose flour (divided), plus extra for dusting
- 1 Tbsp granulated sugar
- 1 tsp salt
- 1 cup (2 sticks) butter, cut into small cubes, chilled
- 1 large egg beaten with 1 Tbsp water, for brushing
- 2 Tbsp turbinado sugar

Chocolate-coated cherries

- 1 heaping cup semi-sweet chocolate chips
- 3 Tbsp butter, cut into 1-inch cubes
- 2 Tbsp light corn syrup
- ⅓ cup stout
- 3 Tbsp heavy cream
- 1 lb dark sweet cherries such as Bing, pitted (see Note)

Topping

- 2 cups heavy cream
- ⅔ cup confectioners' sugar
- 1 tsp vanilla extract or vanilla paste
- 1 cup shaved chocolate (or cocoa powder), or to taste
- 1 to 2 cherries, for garnish

Note: Pitting cherries is a messy job, even with a cherry pitter—the juices stain and it can be incredibly time-consuming. A simple yet effective method is to poke the cherry with a chopstick or a small piping tip, then squeeze out the pit—the cherries will remain intact.

Chocolate-Coated Cherry Pie with Stout

MAKES 1 PIE Jane Wild is that rare combination of pastry chef *and* savory chef, but this heavenly combination of dark chocolate and cherries, subtly flavored with stout beer (Wild is a craft-beer aficionado), strongly favors the baker in her.

Pie crust In a stand mixer fitted with the paddle attachment, combine 1 cup flour, sugar, and salt. Add butter, a little at a time, mixing on low speed. Once all the butter has been added, increase speed to medium and mix until crumbly.

Add the remaining 1 cup flour and mix for 2 to 3 minutes, scraping down the sides of the bowl. Add ¼ cup ice-cold water and mix for another 2 minutes or until dough wraps around the blade like a ball. Transfer dough to a floured work surface and shape it into a ball. Wrap it in plastic wrap and chill for 1 hour in the refrigerator.

Working quickly (so as not to give the butter in the dough a chance to soften), roll out dough to about 12 inches diameter on a floured work surface, then place it in a 9-inch pie plate. Crimp the edges. Using a fork, prick the base, then chill for 20 minutes in the freezer.

Preheat oven to 325°F.

Place a piece of parchment paper over the base of the unbaked crust, then add pie weights, dried beans, or uncooked rice. Bake for 20 to 30 minutes, until crust is lightly golden. Remove pie weights and paper.

Brush the crimped edges with egg wash and sprinkle with turbinado sugar. Bake for another 10 minutes or until crust is golden. Set aside to cool.

Chocolate-covered cherries In the top pan of a double boiler, combine chocolate chips, butter, corn syrup, and stout and set over gently simmering water for 1 to 2 minutes, until chocolate has melted. Stir in cream. Remove from heat.

Add cherries and stir to coat well. Pour mixture into the baked pie crust and refrigerate for at least 4 hours and up to 24 hours, until set.

Topping Prepare the topping just before serving. In a stand mixer fitted with the whisk attachment, whip cream, sugar, and vanilla on high speed for 2 to 3 minutes, until soft peaks form.

Top pie with cream and garnish with shaved chocolate (or dust with cocoa powder). Finish with a cherry or two on top. Pour what's left of the stout into a pint glass and enjoy.

Chocolate-Coated Cherry Pie with Stout | p. 77

Eculent

DAVID SKINNER

⭐ Imagine starting dinner with a tour of a food lab filled with cutting-edge food technology—a 3-D food printer, rotary evaporator ("rotavap"), dehydrators, and freeze-dryers—followed by a view of David Skinner's astonishing collection of house-dried mushrooms, tubers, berries, pollen, herbs, grains, and seaweeds, all stored in neatly labeled containers. Such is the opening scene for diners at Eculent, a cottage restaurant in the heart of historic Kemah. You'll also see a lab larder stocked with house-made infused oils, fruit vinegars, and curing salts, and equipped with hydroponics for microgreens and all the components used in molecular cooking, from sodium alginate to bean gum. "They're derivatives of food, byproducts from fermentation, gums extracted from trees," Skinner explains about the powders he uses to play with the appearance of food, whether it's transforming a liquid into a powder or capturing liquid in a jellified sphere.

At Eculent, you don't just eat a meal. Skinner creates a multisensory dining experience in forty courses. Diners are asked to select "elements" from an altered periodic table to create their own custom drinks. The surface of the counter-seat bar hides a Chinese puzzle box beneath the surface, holding little boxes within that are opened by the chef with a remote control to reveal a course. Cubes of watermelon and tuna on a frozen salt slab look identical. And is that a gem stone? No, it's a humble potato poached in duck fat and coated with ground pistachios (page 82).

Skinner never loses sight of the ultimate dining sense: taste. He cooks with local ingredients, many of which come from the restaurant's garden. Add it all up, and you know why Eculent is one of a kind, and not just in Houston.

▶ **"Gem Stone" Potatoes** | p. 82

3 sprigs rosemary

12 small purple potatoes such as Papa Púrpura, washed and dried

2 to 3 cups duck fat

1 tsp Maldon sea salt

1 cup ground pistachios

¼ cup crème fraîche

Dash of garlic powder

3 to 4 Tbsp caviar (preferably Osetra)

Edible gold leaves (optional)

"Gem Stone" Potatoes

SERVES 4 TO 6 (AS AN APPETIZER) The beauty of this dish is in the simplicity of its preparation. Purple potatoes are poached in duck fat, then coated in ground pistachios. At Eculent, they are served standing up in a miniature "Fabergé" egg, crowned with caviar and gold leaf. Duck fat can be purchased at quality food markets or butchers but, in a pinch, you can use good olive oil instead.

Preheat oven to 225°F.

Place rosemary sprigs on the bottom of a deep baking dish (it should be deep enough for the potatoes to be fully submerged in the duck fat once it's poured in). Add potatoes in a single layer.

In a heavy-bottomed saucepan set over medium-high heat, combine duck fat and salt and heat for 5 minutes or until nearly boiling. Immediately remove the pan from the heat and pour enough duck fat into the baking dish to completely submerge the potatoes. Cover with foil and bake for 1 to 1 ½ hours, until potatoes are tender and can be easily pierced with a knife. Set aside to cool to room temperature.

Increase oven temperature to 300°F. Line a baking sheet with parchment paper.

With your fingers, remove the skins from the potatoes (they should come off very easily). Trim both ends of the potatoes, then trim the potatoes to look like gem stones with facets.

Place ground pistachios in a shallow bowl. Roll potatoes in pistachios and then stand potatoes on the prepared baking sheet. Bake for 10 minutes or until pistachios start to brown. (Do not overcook—you only want to toast the pistachios and warm the potato!)

Meanwhile, combine crème fraîche and garlic powder in a small bowl. Transfer mixture to a piping bag fitted with a small flat tip.

Arrange 2 to 3 potatoes, upright, on individual plates. Pipe a teaspoon of crème fraîche on top of each potato. Top each with caviar and finish with a small piece of gold leaf, if using. Serve immediately.

Carrot soup

3 large carrots, sliced into ¼-inch-thick rounds

½ cup (1 stick) butter

1 tsp salt, plus extra to taste

1 Tbsp lemon juice

Pinch of ground white pepper

Potato soup

2 large russet potatoes, peeled and cut into 1-inch cubes

1 tsp salt, plus extra to taste

1 cup heavy cream

¼ cup (½ stick) butter

1 tsp black pepper, plus extra to taste

½ tsp garlic powder

2 cups milk

Onion soup

1 Tbsp olive oil

2 large white onions, thinly sliced

½ cup heavy cream

½ cup milk

1 Tbsp butter

1¼ tsp salt, plus extra to taste

¼ tsp black pepper, plus extra to taste

2 tsp xanthan gum (optional)

Syringe Soup

SERVES 5 TO 6 Here, three types of soup—each made of simple ingredients that most of us already have in our pantry—are offered together to create a customized experience for each diner. At Eculent, the soups are presented in syringes, but the home cook can easily serve the soups in three separate tureens. Either way, people have the freedom to combine them as they like.

Carrot soup Put carrots, butter, salt, and 2 cups water into a large saucepan set over high heat and heat until the water begins to steam. Reduce heat to medium and cook, covered, for 10 minutes or until carrots are tender.

Transfer carrots to a blender and blend with enough of the cooking liquid to achieve a smooth, thick, and creamy soup. (Reserve some cooking liquid in case you need to adjust the consistency later.) Season with lemon juice, salt and pepper. Keep warm.

Potato soup Place potatoes in a large saucepan, add salt and enough water to cover. Bring to a boil, reduce heat to medium, and cook for 10 minutes or until potatoes are tender enough to be easily pierced with a fork. Drain.

In a blender, combine potatoes, cream, butter, pepper, and garlic powder. Adding milk 1 cup at a time, blend until the mixture has the same consistency as the carrot soup. Season with salt and pepper and keep warm.

Onion soup Heat oil in a large, heavy-bottomed pan over medium heat. Add onions and sauté for 10 to 15 minutes or until softened and translucent (do not allow them to brown). Add cream, milk, butter, and ½ cup water and simmer on low heat for 10 minutes or until thickened.

Transfer mixture to a blender. Season with salt and pepper. Blend until smooth, and keep warm. If you want the soup to have the same consistency as the other two soups, stir in xanthan gum.

Assembly To emulate the chef, fill a 120 ml syringe with each soup base and serve to each guest, along with a soup bowl and this recipe on a card so that they too can create their own soup.

Alternatively, serve the soups in three separate tureens, each with a ladle. Guests can decide for themselves how much of each they want to ladle into their soup bowl.

Fadi's Mediterranean Grill

FADI DIMASSI

⭐ If we eat with our eyes first, then we're feasting at Fadi's. A plethora of mezze on display tempts and woos: silky hummus with caramelized onions and toasted pine nuts, herb-flecked tabbouleh, roasted red muhammara (pepper and walnut dip), and smoky muttabal (eggplant dip). It's easy to fill up on mezze here. Just don't miss out on everything else: the grilled-to-order kebabs, spice-braised lamb shanks, and authentic chicken shawarma are savory essentials on the dining table.

Owner and chef Fadi Dimassi is proud of his American dream. His family came to the U.S. in the nineties seeking refuge from war-torn Lebanon. Growing up in a restaurant family (his parents had a restaurant in Lebanon and later in Houston), Dimassi was well acquainted with the business, working at every restaurant job imaginable—dishwashing, bussing, waiting tables, even valeting.

By 1996, he had saved enough money to open his first restaurant, Yildizlar, which was in many ways the forerunner of what would become his flagship, launched a decade later: Fadi's Mediterranean Grill. Today, Dimassi has four locations in Houston, as well as franchised locations in Dallas.

He still works with his parents. Only now, they work at Fadi's together. All the mezze, meat marinades, and bread doughs are prepared for the various locations at his state-of-the-art commissary kitchen on Highway 6. Why? "With multiple locations, consistency is very important," Dimassi explains.

Imagine, after already finding success in the restaurant business, he decides to get a culinary degree, graduating from the Art Institute of Houston in 2015. "To be a good chef, I want to know not just about Lebanese cuisine but everything else too," he says.

▶ **Fadi's Hummus** | p. 86

Hummus

1¼ cups dried chickpeas, soaked overnight in 2½ cups water

1 tsp baking soda

1 cup tahini

½ Tbsp lemon juice

3 cloves garlic, crushed

1 tsp salt

Caramelized vegetables

1 Tbsp olive oil

1 yellow onion, chopped

Salt and black pepper

¼ green bell pepper, seeded, deveined, and chopped

¼ red bell pepper, seeded, deveined, and chopped

¼ yellow bell pepper, seeded, deveined, and chopped

6 to 8 white button mushrooms, thinly sliced

2 cloves garlic, chopped

2 Tbsp pomegranate molasses

1 tsp ground turmeric

Assembly

1 Tbsp extra-virgin olive oil

1 Tbsp chopped Italian parsley

1 Tbsp chopped mint

Fadi's Hummus

SERVES 8 Of all the hummus on offer, Fadi's version is the most distinguished: it's silky smooth and mixed with mushrooms, peppers, and caramelized onions. The key to that silkiness is blending the ingredients one by one—and trust me, it won't disappoint. In a pinch, you can use canned chickpeas, but still be sure they are soft-boiled so they can be easily smashed between thumb and finger.

Hummus Drain chickpeas, then transfer to a saucepan. Add baking soda and 6 cups water and bring to a boil. Reduce heat to low and keep at a low simmer for 40 to 50 minutes, skimming any foam from the surface, until chickpeas are very tender. (Squeeze one between your finger and thumb: it should turn to mush easily.) Drain and let cool.

In a food processor, process chickpeas on medium speed until they form a stiff paste. With the motor still running, add tahini, lemon juice, garlic, and salt. Continue to mix for 5 minutes while slowly drizzling in ¼ cup ice-cold water. (Add more water if necessary; the hummus should be smooth and creamy.)

Transfer hummus to a bowl, cover with plastic wrap, and set aside.

Caramelized vegetables Heat oil in a large frying pan over medium-high heat. Add onion and a pinch of salt and sauté for 2 to 3 minutes, until onion is softened and translucent. Add bell peppers and cook for another 3 minutes, then reduce heat to medium-low and sauté for 10 minutes. Add mushrooms and cook for 5 minutes. Stir in garlic and sauté for another minute or until fragrant and vegetables are softened and caramelized. Transfer mixture to a bowl and let cool.

Reserve 1 to 2 tablespoons of the mixture for garnish. To the remaining mixture, stir in pomegranate molasses and turmeric. Season with salt and pepper. Set aside.

Assembly Add the caramelized vegetables to the bowl of hummus. Drizzle with olive oil and garnish with the reserved caramelized vegetables, parsley, and mint.

Or, for an elevated plating, follow Chef Dimassi's lead and place a ring mold in the center of a plate, line it with thinly sliced cucumber and carrot, fill with hummus, and arrange garnish on top. Remove the ring mold before serving.

Caramelized onions

2 Tbsp vegetable oil

2 large yellow onions, thinly sliced

Tahini sauce

2 cups Caramelized Onions (see here)

1 cup tahini

1 cup orange juice

1 cup mandarin juice

½ cup lemon juice

2 tsp pomegranate molasses

1 tsp ground cumin

1 tsp salt

½ tsp chili flakes

Tahini-baked salmon

2 lbs fresh skin-on salmon fillet, cleaned

1 tsp salt

1 tsp black pepper

2 Tbsp olive oil

2 cups Tahini Sauce (see here)

½ cup chopped mint

½ cup chopped Italian parsley

¼ cup chopped walnuts

¼ red bell pepper, seeded, deveined, and finely chopped

Tahini-Baked Salmon

SERVES 4 TO 5 In 2017, Fadi Dimassi won the tenth annual Zest in the West culinary competition with his tahini-baked fish. He used branzino, but the dish also works with salmon, steelhead trout fillet, or try flounder. The tahini sauce, rich with caramelized onions, fresh citrus, and spices, is everything to this dish.

Caramelized onions Heat oil in a large frying pan over medium heat. Add onions and sauté for 10 to 15 minutes, until softened and caramelized. Don't let them burn or brown.

Tahini sauce In a blender or food processor, blend all ingredients until smooth.

Tahini-baked salmon Preheat oven to 375°F.

Place salmon, skin-side down, on a piece of parchment paper large enough to fold over the fish. Season fish with salt and pepper and drizzle oil overtop. Fold the edges of the parchment paper over the fish and seal into a packet.

Place fish on a baking sheet on the bottom rack of the oven and bake for 25 minutes or until salmon is cooked through and flaky. (Or until the internal temperature reaches 145°F on an instant-read thermometer.)

Assembly Carefully unfold the parchment paper to let the steam escape, and open up the packet. Serve the fish in the parchment or transfer it to a serving platter. Spoon tahini sauce overtop, then garnish with mint, parsley, walnuts, and bell pepper.

Field & Tides

TRAVIS LENIG

★ The charming twenties cottage restaurant on 11th Street has a timeless sense of hospitality and contemporary Gulf Coast–meets–Hill Country ambiance. With its original dark wood floor from 1936 and eye-catching antler-entwined chandelier, it's a cozy space. From the dining room you can see through to the semi-open kitchen, and the chef often pops in to say hello to guests. This is Field & Tides, and it's everything chef Travis Lenig imagined it to be. It's a chef's dream to own their own restaurant, and Lenig owns his with pizzazz.

Field & Tides is a play on the surf-and-turf theme; you'll find everything from molasses-lacquered duck and juniper-spiced venison to oysters on the half shell to seared scallops with shrimp and crab risotto. When Lenig says he sources locally, he means very close to home indeed: "A lot of our produce comes from my wife's family farm in Round Top," he says. "They tell me what they're planting, so I can plan my menu around it."

On a beautiful day, the patio invites you to sit at one of the handcrafted wooden tables. Enjoy a cocktail and crispy-fried green tomatoes, or a bowl of pimento cheese fritters, served with a dollop of pepper jelly. It's a perfect lunchtime spot to try the imaginative Sloppy Tides, a balancing act of crusty Gulf fish supporting a runny fried egg, chipotle mayo, and pickled slaw on a fluffy challah bun. Lenig is a native Houstonian. His food is rooted in Southern cuisine, but as a true Houston chef, he draws on influences from other cuisines, ensuring that Field & Tides has something for everyone.

Pork belly

1 to 2 Tbsp canola oil

1 (3-lb) skinless pork belly

Salt and black pepper

1 onion, roughly chopped

Head of garlic, cloves separated, peeled, and crushed

Sprig of thyme, leaves chopped

Sprig of rosemary, leaves chopped

Guajillo sauce

3 guajillo chiles, seeded

2 Tbsp honey

2 Tbsp sherry vinegar

¼ cup olive oil

Salt and black pepper

Sweet potato hash

3 sweet potatoes, peeled and chopped

Sprig of thyme, leaves only

3 Tbsp canola oil (divided)

Salt and black pepper

2 poblano peppers

2 red bell peppers

1 large red onion, thinly sliced

Pork Belly with Sweet Potato Hash and Guajillo Sauce

SERVES 4 Roast pork belly made a day in advance means you'll be ready to sizzle up this homerun brunch in next to no time. Roasted peppers and sweet potatoes make for a hearty marriage, bound together with the rustic heat of guajillo pepper sauce.

Pork belly Preheat oven to 300°F. Rub oil over pork belly and generously season with salt and pepper.

Scatter onion on the bottom of a roasting pan large enough to fit the pork belly. Place pork belly on the onion and arrange garlic, thyme, and rosemary on top. Add enough water to cover the bottom of the pan (not the belly) and cover with foil. Roast for 4 hours or until belly is tender and nicely browned. Set aside to cool to room temperature.

Guajillo sauce Soak peppers in a bowl of hot water for 15 minutes or until softened. Reserve 1 tablespoon soaking liquid.

In a blender, pulse chiles, reserved soaking liquid, honey, and vinegar to blend. With the motor running on medium speed, slowly pour in oil until emulsified. Season with salt and pepper. Set aside.

Sweet potato hash Preheat oven to 400°F.

In a large bowl, gently toss sweet potatoes with thyme and 1 tablespoon oil to coat. Season with salt and pepper. Transfer to a baking sheet and roast for 10 to 15 minutes, until potatoes are cooked through and soft. Set aside.

Brush poblano and bell peppers with 1 tablespoon oil and place on a baking sheet. Roast for 15 to 20 minutes, until charred and blistered all over. Transfer peppers to a plastic bag and let sit for 10 minutes to loosen the skin. When cool enough to handle, remove skins, stems, and seeds (do not rinse under the tap). Slice into thin strips.

Heat the remaining 1 tablespoon oil in a frying pan over medium-high heat. Add onion and sauté for 5 to 8 minutes, until caramelized. Add sliced peppers, and set aside.

Assembly

2 Tbsp canola oil (divided)

4 large eggs, cooked to
preference

Handful of cilantro leaves

¼ cup crumbled
queso fresco

Sliced serrano peppers
(optional)

Assembly Heat 1 tablespoon oil in a frying pan over medium-high heat. Add the sweet potatoes and cook for 2 minutes. Add ¼ cup guajillo sauce and cook for another 2 to 3 minutes. Add the caramelized onion and roasted peppers mixture, and cook for 1 minute, to heat everything through. Season with salt and pepper.

Slice the pork belly into 4 equal portions.

Heat the remaining 1 tablespoon oil in a separate frying pan over medium-high heat. Add pork belly and brown for 1 minute on each side.

Spoon the sweet potato hash into warm bowls and top with slices of pork belly. Place an egg on the pork slices (1 egg per bowl) and drizzle guajillo sauce overtop. Garnish with cilantro, queso fresco, and sliced serrano peppers, if using. Serve immediately.

Poblano mash

3 russet potatoes, peeled and cut into 2-inch cubes

2 poblano peppers

½ bunch cilantro

¼ cup spinach

Salt and black pepper

1 cup heavy cream, room temperature

½ cup (1 stick) butter, room temperature

Braised red cabbage

¼ cup canola oil

1 large red onion, thinly sliced

1 head red cabbage, cored and thinly sliced

1 cinnamon stick

1 vanilla bean, split lengthwise, pods removed and stem saved

½ cup red wine vinegar

¼ cup brown sugar

Salt and black pepper

Bourbon reduction

1 Tbsp butter

1 shallot, finely chopped

1 clove garlic, finely chopped

1 cup bourbon

3 cups demi-glace (see Note)

Salt and black pepper

Venison, Poblano Mash, Red Cabbage, and Bourbon Reduction

SERVES 4 Venison seasoned with juniper berries and served with sweet-sour braised red cabbage and roasted poblano and cilantro mash potatoes is a Field & Tides favorite. Look for venison at D'artagnan, Katerra Exotics, or Broken Arrow Ranch (which is where chef Lenig sources his venison). Alternatively? Veal chops and rib-eye steak love this combination, too!

Poblano mash Place potatoes in a saucepan of cold water and bring to a boil over medium-high heat. Reduce heat to medium and cook for 10 minutes or until tender. Drain.

Meanwhile, roast poblano peppers over an open flame on the stove for 5 to 10 minutes, turning regularly, until softened and charred. (Alternatively, roast them in a 400°F oven for 20 minutes or until softened and blistered.) Transfer peppers to a plastic bag and let sit for 10 minutes to loosen the skin. When cool enough to handle, remove skin, stem, and seeds (do not rinse under the tap).

In a small blender, purée peppers, cilantro, spinach, and salt and pepper to taste. (Add a little water as needed, to get it going).

Mash potatoes and return them to the pan. Add cream and butter and mash until smooth. Using a spatula, mix in the poblano mixture. Season with salt and pepper. Keep warm.

Braised red cabbage Heat oil in a large Dutch oven over medium heat. Add onion and sauté for 3 minutes. Add cabbage and cook for 4 minutes, stirring occasionally. Add cinnamon and vanilla and cook for another 4 minutes.

Stir in vinegar and cook for 5 minutes. Add sugar and stir until dissolved. Season with salt and pepper. Keep warm.

Bourbon reduction Melt butter in a saucepan over medium-high heat. Add shallot and garlic and cook for 1 minute. Reduce heat to medium-low and add bourbon, a little at a time, stirring continuously. Increase heat to medium and cook

Venison

4 juniper berries

2 Tbsp kosher salt

1 rack of venison
(4 double-bone venison
loin chops), cleaned
and frenched

2 Tbsp canola oil

Black pepper

for 5 to 8 minutes, until bourbon is reduced by half. (Adding bourbon in one go may result in a flambé—if it does, stay cool and let the bourbon do its job; the flame will die out.) Add demi-glace and cook for another 10 to 15 minutes, until reduced by a quarter. Season with salt and pepper. Keep warm.

Venison Preheat oven to 350°F.

Heat a small frying pan over high heat. Toast juniper berries for 30 seconds or until fragrant. Using a mortar and pestle, crush the berries to a coarse powder. Transfer to a small bowl and mix with salt.

Coat rack in oil, then generously season with juniper salt and pepper. (You should be able to smell the juniper.)

Heat a heavy-bottomed ovenproof frying pan over high heat until nearly smoking. Holding the rack by the bone, place it in the pan. Sear for 1 minute. Turn over and sear for another minute or until golden brown. Place the pan in the oven and roast for 25 to 30 minutes for medium-rare. Transfer

rack to a cutting board, loosely tent with foil, and let rest for 10 to 15 minutes.

Assembly Cut the venison rack into individual chops. Spoon ½ cup each of poblano mash and braised cabbage onto warmed plates. Lean the chops up against the mash, crossing the bones. Drizzle bourbon reduction around each plate and serve immediately.

Note: Demi-glace (traditionally veal glaze) is a gourmet item that can be found at fine food stores or Central Market, or via Amazon. Alternatively, use a good-quality beef stock and thicken with a little cornstarch.

Venison, Poblano Mash, Red Cabbage, and Bourbon Reduction | p. 92–93

Giacomo's Cibo e Vino

LYNETTE HAWKINS

⭐ Giacomo's Cibo e Vino may be on busy Westheimer Road, but it has all the charm of a neighborhood restaurant, with friends sharing convivial meals, kids happily slurping house-made pastas, and dogs lazing at the foot of tables on the shaded patio.

The bungalow restaurant, opened in 2009, is the domain of owner-chef Lynette Hawkins. Hawkins spent her formative years in Italy, where the flavors of ingredient-driven Italian cuisine forever lodged in her soul. She was raised on seasonality and eating local, and that remains at the core of her cooking today. At Hawkins's trattoria, fresh pastas are made with Ole Dad Farm eggs, and any *maltagliati* (irregular pasta cuts) go into a bean and tomato soup. That pork shoulder, rubbed with fennel and slowly roasted, comes from Black Hill Meats. Texas Longhorn Cattle & Land Co. has provided her with Longhorn beef since she first rolled her *polpetti* (page 100). Knopp Branch Farm vegetables, which shine in seasonal soups, sides, and salads, are delivered to the kitchen door by the farmer himself.

Whatever you order here, don't overlook the *cicchetti*, the small hot and cold dishes. "I love to see people sharing and trying different things," Hawkins says. "I like to eat this way, and I am so glad that my customers enjoy it too!" Favorites include succulent shrimp in house-made harissa (mop it up with crusty bread); grilled radicchio stuffed with roasted pepper, prosciutto, and melted mozzarella; and the savory-sweet caramelized onion and goat cheese tart. And Hawkins is right. Food, even food this good, tastes better when shared with friends and family.

▶ **Ravioli with Swiss Chard, Ricotta, and Goat Cheese in Sage Butter Sauce** | p. 98–99

Pasta dough

3 cups durum flour, plus extra for dusting

4 free-range eggs, lightly beaten

4 free-range egg yolks, lightly beaten

Filling

2 bunches Swiss chard, leaves only, roughly chopped

2 Tbsp butter

2 Tbsp olive oil

1 large shallot, finely chopped

Salt and black pepper

1 large egg

⅔ cup grated Parmesan

½ cup creamy goat cheese

½ cup ricotta

Pinch of freshly grated nutmeg

Stuffed pasta

Durum flour, for dusting

1 tsp salt

Filling (see here)

Semolina flour, for sprinkling

Ravioli with Swiss Chard, Ricotta, and Goat Cheese in Sage Butter Sauce

SERVES 4 Making your own pasta feels good. You'll feel a great sense of accomplishment when you cut circles from your own dough and later see your ravioli hold their shape upon boiling. At Giacomo's, chef Lynette Hawkins uses durum flour rather than "oo" flour. It yields a sturdier, more toothsome pasta, and it's less likely to fall apart, making it perfect for stuffing.

Pasta dough In a food processor, combine flour, eggs, and egg yolks, pulsing for 2 to 3 minutes, until dough comes together in small clumps. Transfer dough to a floured work surface and knead for 5 minutes into a smooth ball. Cover with plastic wrap and let rest for 30 minutes.

Filling Bring a large saucepan of water to a boil and add a pinch of salt. Add Swiss chard and cook for 30 seconds, then drain and let cool.

Heat butter and oil in a large frying pan over medium-high heat. Add shallot, season with a pinch of salt, and sauté for 3 to 4 minutes, until softened and slightly caramelized.

Squeeze the blanched Swiss chard to remove the excess liquid, add to the pan, and cook for 2 to 3 minutes. Remove from heat and let cool. Transfer mixture to a cutting board and finely chop.

In a large mixing bowl, combine the chard mixture, egg, Parmesan, goat cheese, ricotta, and nutmeg. Season with salt and pepper.

Stuffed pasta Divide dough into 2 pieces. On a floured work surface, roll each piece into a ½-inch-thick rectangle as wide as the pasta machine roller. Roll a piece through the pasta machine at the thickest setting, usually #1. Sprinkle dough with durum flour, then fold into thirds like a letter. Run dough through this setting again. Repeat this process two or three more times, until pasta is smooth, silky, and not at all sticky.

Continue rolling dough through each setting until you reach #6. Make sure to dust dough with durum flour each time you roll it and change the setting. You should end up with a 5-foot sheet of pasta. Repeat with the other piece of dough.

Assembly

½ cup (1 stick) butter (divided)

1 Tbsp olive oil

10 sage leaves

1 Tbsp finely chopped shallots

Salt and black pepper

Grated Parmesan, for sprinkling

> **Note:** Keep those ravioli cuttings. You can cut them into your own maltagliati (odd-shaped) pasta. Or you can reknead the dough and repeat the process of rolling it out in the pasta machine to make sheets or fettuccine, for instance.

Sprinkle semolina flour over the pasta, then fold it in half so it measures 2½ feet. Sprinkle a little more semolina on top and fold pasta in half again. (It's important to dust with semolina between layers to prevent them from sticking. You will have 4 layers in total.) With a 2½-inch cookie cutter, cut out circles.

Place a heaping teaspoon of filling in the center of each pasta round. Using your index finger, moisten edges with a little water. Fold over dough to form a semicircle and, using your index finger and thumb, press along the edges to seal.

Bring a large saucepan of water to a boil and add salt. Working in batches to avoid overcrowding, carefully lower in ravioli using a slotted spoon. Cook for 3 to 4 minutes, until ravioli float to the surface. Using a slotted spoon, transfer ravioli to a colander and drain. Repeat with the remaining ravioli. Reserve ½ cup pasta water.

Assembly Heat ¼ cup (½ stick) butter and oil in a large frying pan over medium-high heat. Add sage and cook for 1 to 2 minutes, until crispy. Set aside 1 or 2 leaves, for garnish. Add shallots and cook for another 3 minutes or until tender. Season with salt and pepper.

Add ravioli and the remaining ¼ cup (½ stick) butter. Stir in 1 to 2 tablespoons pasta water, swirling pan until creamy and emulsified. (Add more pasta water as needed.) Transfer to a serving plate, sprinkle with Parmesan, garnish with the reserved sage, and serve immediately.

Brodo

2 lbs chicken scraps and bones

½ lb oxtail or beef bones with meat

1 large turkey neck

2 chicken feet

1 large yellow onion, roughly chopped

1 carrot, roughly chopped

1 stalk celery, roughly chopped

2 cloves garlic

8 sprigs Italian parsley

2 sprigs thyme

1 bay leaf

2 tsp tomato paste

2 tsp kosher salt

Fennel-and-onion confit

1 large fennel bulb, cored and thinly sliced on a mandolin (about 1 cup)

1 red onion, thinly sliced on a mandolin (about 1 cup)

1½ cups olive oil

½ Tbsp kosher salt

1 star anise

Polpetti Puccini

SERVES 4 TO 6 Nothing speaks of comfort like classic meatballs. This version sees them made with Longhorn beef. Why Longhorn? This pasture-raised breed's meat is healthy, low in saturated fat, and leaner than most other beef. It can be found at local farmers' markets. If you're pressed for time, replace the brodo with 1 cup quality chicken stock and 1 cup quality beef stock.

Brodo Put chicken bones, oxtail (or beef bones), turkey neck, chicken feet, and 1 gallon cold water into a large stockpot and bring to a low boil over medium heat. Simmer for 30 minutes, skimming off any foam from the surface. Add the remaining ingredients, cover, and gently simmer over low heat for 6 to 8 hours. (Alternatively, simmer in a crockpot set on low.)

Strain brodo through a colander into a large bowl and let cool completely. (You can also place the bowl in an ice bath.) Cover and refrigerate overnight. The following day, remove the solidified fat from the surface and discard.

Fennel-and-onion confit In a saucepan, bring all ingredients to a slow boil over medium heat. Reduce heat to medium-low and, stirring occasionally, gently simmer for 1 hour or until vegetables are softened and translucent. Set aside to cool to room temperature. Discard star anise. (Makes about 4 cups.)

Using a slotted spoon, scoop the fennel-onion confit into a clean jar or other container. Pour in enough of the oil from the fennel-onion confit to submerge mixture and cover with a lid. (Confit can be stored in an airtight container in the refrigerator up to 1 month. Add leftovers to tomato sauce, bean stews, or braised pork.)

Puccini meatballs In a large bowl, combine breadcrumbs and milk, making sure breadcrumbs are completely soaked.

Heat oil in a large frying pan over medium heat. Add onion and 1 teaspoon salt and sauté for 5 minutes or until onion is softened. Add garlic, reduce heat to medium-low, and sauté for another 5 minutes or until onion is caramelized.

Puccini meatballs

1 cup breadcrumbs

½ cup milk

2 Tbsp olive oil, plus extra for brushing

1 large yellow onion, finely chopped

2 tsp kosher salt (divided)

2 to 3 cloves garlic, finely chopped

¼ cup dry red wine

1 Tbsp fennel seeds

1 tsp chili flakes

½ tsp black peppercorns

1 large egg, beaten

½ cup grated Parmesan

⅓ cup finely chopped Italian parsley

¼ cup finely chopped basil

1 lb ground beef (preferably Texas Longhorn beef) or bison

½ lb ground pastured pork

Assembly

¼ heaping cup Fennel-and-Onion Confit (see here)

25 to 30 Puccini Meatballs (see here)

2 cups Brodo (see here)

2 cups tomato sauce

2 Tbsp heavy cream

Cooked pasta or roasted potatoes, to serve

Stir in wine and cook for 2 minutes or until the wine has evaporated. Remove from heat and let cool.

Heat a small frying pan over high heat for 1 minute. Toast fennel seeds, chili flakes, and peppercorns for 1 minute or until they start to pop. Using a mortar and pestle, grind to a powder.

To the bowl of soaked breadcrumbs, add the onion mixture, egg, Parmesan, herbs, remaining 1 teaspoon salt, and ground spices. Add beef (or bison) and pork and mix gently to thoroughly combine.

Preheat oven to 350°F. Brush a baking sheet with oil and set aside.

To test the seasoning, take a tablespoon of mixture and form it into a patty. In a nonstick frying pan, fry the patty for 3 to 4 minutes, until cooked through. Taste, then season mixture with salt as needed. Shape the mixture into golf ball–size meatballs. (Makes 25 to 30.)

Place meatballs on the prepared baking sheet and roast for 20 to 25 minutes, until cooked and golden.

Assembly In a large frying pan over medium-high heat, heat the confit and meatballs. Using a wooden spoon, stir for 2 minutes or until meatballs are browned. Pour in brodo and bring to a boil. Reduce heat to medium-low and simmer for 5 minutes or until meatballs are heated through. Stir in tomato sauce and cream and simmer for 3 minutes or until hot.

Serve over pasta or with roasted potatoes.

Ginger & Fork

MARY LI

★ How often do you find yourself at a Chinese restaurant trying to decide between Peking duck bao or cha siu sliders, then figuring out the appropriate craft cocktail to pair it with? Well, that's standard at this charming black-and-white cottage on Inker Street.

Ginger & Fork is the best way to taste Hong Kong in Houston. As soon as you walk in, the long marbled bar beckons to you for predinner drinks and a friendly chat with the bartender. Enjoy a signature cocktail such as the fresh Ginger Margarita with traditional fare like crispy squid tossed with sautéed onions and peppers. And the matchmaking continues at the table: smoky notes of ancho pepper in the spicy Dragon Fire cocktail (page 104) complement the mellow umami of beef chow fun (page 103), while a rum-based Panama Daiquiri, made with sugar cane and eucalyptus, pairs nicely with steamed dumplings. There are also great wines on offer, to pair with delicate seabass steamed with ginger and scallions, or with sizzling beef with charred onions in black pepper sauce.

Owner and mixologist Mary Li, who shook and stirred the bar program at Houston's Tony Mandola's for over two decades, opened Ginger & Fork to combine her two loves under one roof: cocktails and Cantonese cuisine. "With Chinese food, you usually go just to eat," says Li. "I added a craft cocktail and wine program so that our guests can have a full dining experience." With the restaurant located just off South Shepherd in Houston's Inner Loop, Li also dispels the belief that one must travel to Chinatown for authentic Chinese food.

Cap off the meal with warm Asian pear bread pudding drizzled with bourbon caramel or Li's ambrosial ginger parfait. From cocktails to desserts, Ginger & Fork elevates Chinese food to a fine-dining experience.

Marinated beef

1 Tbsp soy sauce

1 tsp rice cooking wine (preferably Shaoxing)

1 tsp powdered chicken stock

½ tsp cornstarch

¼ tsp granulated sugar

¼ tsp salt

4½ oz beef sirloin, sliced thinly

Beef chow fun

2 Tbsp vegetable oil

Marinated Beef (see here)

¼ yellow onion, thinly sliced

10 oz flat rice noodles, cooked and separated

Pinch of salt

Pinch of granulated sugar

Pinch of powdered chicken stock

1 tsp soy sauce

3 scallions, cut into 2-inch pieces

1 cup bean sprouts

Beef Chow Fun

SERVES 2 TO 4 This dish is usually ordered as part of a family-style meal. Chow fun—a flat rice noodle with a chewy and rather slippery texture—is the star of the dish, here enhanced by beef sirloin. To make this a standalone meal, add more sirloin.

Marinated beef In a bowl, combine soy sauce, cooking wine, powdered stock, cornstarch, sugar, and salt. Add beef and let sit for 30 minutes to marinate.

Beef chow fun Heat oil in a wok or large frying pan over high heat. Add beef slices and stir-fry for 15 seconds. Transfer to a plate and set aside.

Drain oil from pan, leaving only a coating of it. Heat pan over high heat until nearly smoking. Add onion and stir-fry for 30 seconds. Add noodles and stir to prevent them from sticking to the wok. Add beef and marinade and stir for 10 seconds. Season with salt, sugar, powdered stock, and soy sauce. Stir in scallions and bean sprouts and stir-fry for another 30 seconds or until noodles are golden brown and evenly coated.

Transfer to a serving plate and serve immediately.

Simple syrup

1 cup granulated sugar

Dragon fire

1½ oz Tanqueray Rangpur

1 oz red dragon fruit, mashed

¾ oz lime juice

¾ oz Simple Syrup (see here)

¾ Ancho Reyes Ancho Chile Liqueur

3 dashes bitter (preferably Bad Dog Bar Craft Fire and Damnation Bitters)

Icy-cold cocktail coupe

Note: You can also use a cobbler shaker, a three-part shaker with cap and strainer.

Dragon Fire Cocktail

SERVES 1 When it comes to spicy cocktails, Ginger & Fork is well ahead of the curve. Fresh ginger and citrus are common ingredients in its concoctions, and this bright and beautifully balanced cocktail is a restaurant favorite. It's made with Ancho Reyes (a Mexican liqueur made with ancho seeds) and a bitter crafted with habanero, black tea, and molasses. If you like, you can use a bitter from your personal bar collection instead.

Simple syrup In a saucepan, combine sugar and 1 cup water and heat through until sugar is dissolved. Set aside to cool to room temperature. (Leftover syrup can be stored in a jar in the refrigerator for up to 1 month.)

Dragon fire Put all ingredients in the small tin of a Boston shaker (see Note), then fill it with ice cubes. Close shaker and shake for 15 to 20 seconds.

Using a Hawthorne strainer, strain mixture into the frozen glass. Use a julep strainer to scoop away excess ice floating on top, then serve.

Harlem Road BBQ

ARA MALEKIAN

⭐ Harlem Road BBQ may be located on Houston's west side (or "long distance" for Inner Loop Houstonians), but the craft barbecue is worth the drive. Even fans from Austin and San Antonio know it! Pitmaster Ara Malekian fires up his smoker with wine barrel staves for "extra aroma" and adds grounds of Armenian coffee to his dry rub.

The brisket is juicy and tender, the sausages are made in-house, and the ribs are sticky and delicious, yet Harlem Road BBQ offers so much more than the traditional Texas trinity of barbecue. Spiced-up beef cheek *barbacoa* smolders with smoky flavor, while Gulf fish are hot-smoked over dried grapevines. Malekian will even smoke bourbon-brushed oyster mushrooms or octopus glazed with pomegranate reduction. And when available, the smoked T-bone and rack of lamb are must-orders.

Malekian is Armenian and speaks seven languages. His cooking skills are almost as varied—Malekian draws inspiration from both classic French cuisine and recipes that trace back to his early childhood in Iran. As Wolfgang Puck's corporate chef between 2000 and 2006, Malekian opened back-to-back restaurants, including two of his own in San Francisco. But eventually he wanted a change of pace, and the low and slow of barbecue was the ticket: "I love cooking with fire and wood and smoke," he shares. "It's primal," adding that barbecue requires its own skillset—from trimming brisket to controlling the smoke temperature.

So Malekian left the corporate restaurant world and opened Harlem Road BBQ, designing the restaurant himself—a vaulted space artfully lined with old fence wood and oozing with rustic country-cabin charm under the big Texas sky. The rural plot has its perks, says Malekian: "I don't have nearby neighbors. If I want to roast a whole animal, I can do it outside, carve, and serve until I run out."

▶ **Smoked Lamb Chops with Caramelized Onions** | p. 109

1 rack of lamb, frenched

1 white onion, halved
   and thinly sliced

1 Tbsp coarse salt,
   or to taste

1 Tbsp black pepper

1 Tbsp sumac

1 Tbsp butter

Smoked Lamb Chops with Caramelized Onions

SERVES 2 TO 3 These finger-licking-good lamb chops burst with big flavor, thanks to an overnight marinade and, of course, a smoker. Many Texan home cooks have a backyard smoker, and the key to this recipe's success is maintaining the right temperature. If you don't have one, you can prepare these chops on a coal or gas barbecue. They may not have that smoky dimension, but they will be nicely charred. At Harlem Road BBQ, you have a choice of house-made sides; at home, serve these chops with a side of mash and grilled asparagus.

Place lamb chops in a shallow dish and scatter onion on top. Cover with plastic wrap and refrigerate overnight.

Preheat smoker to 235°F.

Remove rack of lamb from the refrigerator and set aside to warm to room temperature. Transfer onion to a bowl and reserve. Season lamb with salt, pepper, and sumac. Smoke for 1 to 1½ hours, or until the internal temperature of the meat reaches 135°F on an instant-read thermometer. Set aside lamb for 20 minutes.

Meanwhile, melt butter in a large frying pan over medium heat. Add onion, reduce heat to medium-low, and sauté for 10 minutes or until caramelized.

Carve lamb into individual chops, then serve with caramelized onions.

Bread pudding

Butter, for greasing

6 cups cubed day-old croissant or brioche (1-inch pieces)

3 cups heavy cream

1 cup finely chopped semi-sweet chocolate

¼ cup prepared Armenian coffee or espresso

1 cup granulated sugar

½ cup tightly packed light brown sugar

6 large eggs

1 Tbsp vanilla extract

Bourbon-caramel sauce

½ cup granulated sugar

6 Tbsp butter, cut into cubes

2 Tbsp bourbon

1 cup heavy cream

Chocolate Bread Pudding with Bourbon-Caramel Sauce

SERVES 6 TO 8 Chocolate bread pudding truly is the sweetest ending to any hearty meal. The "secret" ingredient in this particular recipe is the Armenian coffee, which adds incredible depth of flavor. Traditionally, Armenian coffee, or *soorj*, is prepared in a handheld coffee maker known as a *jazzve*. In lieu of Armenian coffee, you can use espresso.

Bread pudding Preheat oven to 325°F. Lightly grease a 9- × 13-inch baking pan and add croissant (or brioche) cubes.

Bring cream to a low simmer in a saucepan. Stir in chocolate and coffee, and mix until melted.

In a bowl, combine both sugars. Stir in chocolate mixture, then set aside to cool.

In a large bowl, lightly beat eggs and vanilla to combine. Slowly pour in the cooled cream mixture, gently whisking to mix. Pour mixture over croissant cubes and, stirring occasionally, let sit for 20 minutes or until bread has absorbed most of the mixture. Bake for 1 hour or until a knife inserted into the center comes out clean.

Bourbon-caramel sauce Warm sugar in a heavy-bottomed saucepan over medium-high heat until sugar begins to melt. Whisk gently until sugar is dissolved and turns amber. Reduce heat to medium-low and immediately add butter and whisk until melted and thoroughly combined.

Stir in bourbon and cook over low heat for 1 minute. Remove pan from heat. Slowly pour in cream, whisking until smooth. Keep hot, or reheat when needed.

Assembly Cut the warm bread pudding into squares, arrange on plates, and drizzle hot bourbon-caramel sauce overtop. Serve immediately.

Harold's Restaurant and Tap Room

ALLI JARRETT

★ Across the street from the vintage Heights Theater, Harold's Restaurant and Tap Room retains the historic charm of a bygone era. The building, previously housing long-established garment department store Harolds, was transformed by owner Alli Jarrett into a multiconcept restaurant that preserves the cultural heritage of the space. With former chef Antoine Ware in the kitchen for the first four years, Harold's immediately established itself as a destination for fine Southern food.

Jarrett expanded with a food truck in 2017 and the seafood restaurant Low Tide in Finn Hall in 2018, around the same time that she celebrated Harold's fifth birthday.

The talented and hard-working executive chef (and Texas native) Kathy Elkins joined the team in the spring of 2018. She knows how to bring it. Her playful and refreshing flavors are rooted in Southern cuisine: roasted Texas quail is served with cabbage and fennel stippled with hearty bacon and pickled raisins. A seasonal peach salad (page 114)—with herbs, jalapeño, creamy feta, crispy-fried shallots, and blueberry-balsamic reduction—is an all-round winner, as is the flavor-packed Southern-smoked short rib saddled on smoky Gouda grits.

Although the menu changes regularly, Harold's always offers classic Southern comfort food: deeply flavored dark chicken and sausage gumbo, perfectly Southern fried Whitehurst Farm chicken, and big and juicy Gulf shrimp and creamy grits (page 113). Jarrett and Elkins share an appreciation for honest Southern dishes made with fresh, locally sourced ingredients. "Kathy is a country girl, just like me," says Jarrett. "Her hush puppies remind me of my childhood."

Grits

2 cups stone-ground yellow grits

2 cups shredded white cheddar

½ cup heavy cream

1 large egg

Salt and black pepper

Shrimp-and-grits sauce

1 cup Worcestershire sauce

¼ cup lemon juice

2 cups heavy cream

1 tsp Creole seasoning

Salt and black pepper

Assembly

20 large (10/15) Gulf shrimp, peeled with tails intact

10 slices bacon, halved lengthwise

1 small yellow onion, finely chopped

3 cloves garlic, finely chopped

4 to 6 oyster mushrooms, sliced

2 cups Shrimp-and-Grits Sauce (see here)

¼ cup (½ stick) butter, cold

Shrimp and Grits

SERVES 4 TO 5 Sweet Gulf shrimps are snuggled in a zingy sauce that jolts this dish into the upper echelons of Southern cooking. Start with quality, stone-ground grits (Harold's uses grits from Homestead Gristmill in Waco, Texas). When cooked, the coarsely textured grits transform into a toothsome porridge with a distinct corn flavor. And you ought to make a double batch of the sauce—it's *that* good.

Grits Bring 2 quarts of water to a boil in a large, heavy-bottomed saucepan. Gradually add grits while stirring continuously with a wooden spoon. Bring mixture to a boil, then reduce heat to low and cover. Simmer for 15 to 20 minutes, stirring occasionally, until water is absorbed and the grits are thick.

Slowly stir in the cheddar, cream, and egg and cook for another 20 to 25 minutes, until thick and creamy. Season with salt and pepper. Keep warm.

Shrimp-and-grits sauce In a medium saucepan, combine Worcestershire sauce and lemon juice and bring to a boil. Reduce heat to medium and cook for 10 minutes or until sauce is reduced by half and thick enough to coat the back of a spoon.

Pour in cream and cook over medium-high heat for 5 minutes or until reduced by a third. Stir in Creole seasoning and season with salt and pepper. (If your Creole seasoning contains salt, be careful not to over-salt.) Keep warm.

Assembly Wrap each shrimp with a piece of bacon.

Heat a frying pan over high heat. Put shrimp into pan, reduce heat to medium-high, and sauté for 5 to 7 minutes, until bacon is crisp and shrimp are cooked through. Transfer to a plate and keep warm.

Drain all but 1 tablespoon bacon fat from the pan. Place pan over medium heat, add onion, garlic, and mushrooms, and sauté for 3 to 5 minutes, until softened. Pour in the sauce and cook for another 1 to 2 minutes to heat through. Just before serving, stir in the cold butter.

Spoon grits onto the center of individual plates and ladle sauce all around. Arrange shrimp around grits and top with onion-mushroom mixture. Serve immediately.

Blueberry-balsamic reduction

1 cup blueberries

4 cups balsamic vinegar

3 Tbsp granulated sugar

½ tsp salt

Crispy-fried shallots

½ cup rice flour

4 shallots, thinly sliced

Canola or peanut oil, for deep-frying

Salt

Peach salad

2 large ripe peaches, peeled and cut into 1-inch cubes

¼ tsp Tajin seasoning (see Note)

Pinch of salt

¼ cup Blueberry-Balsamic Reduction (see here)

Handful of mint leaves, torn

Handful of cilantro leaves, torn

½ jalapeño pepper, seeded and very thinly sliced

2 oz creamy feta, crumbled

1 cup Crispy-Fried Shallots (see here)

¼ tsp lemon juice

Peach, Herb, and Feta Salad

SERVES 4 Every summer, Fredericksburg becomes the seasonal capital of Texas peaches. You'll find peach stalls at every turn, set up at orchards and roadsides across the region. Farmers' markets in Houston swell with the seasonal presence of peach vendors. "Peach is my favorite stone fruit," says Kathy Elkins. "There is something about that sweet, soft yet firm flesh wrapped in baby fuzz. I wanted this seasonal salad to be treasured while it's on the menu and missed when it's not."

Blueberry-balsamic reduction Place all ingredients in a saucepan and bring to a slow boil over medium-high heat, stirring occasionally with a wooden spoon to prevent the bottom from burning. Reduce heat to medium and gently simmer for 10 to 15 minutes, until syrupy and reduced by half. Strain through a fine-mesh sieve into a bowl and let cool. Pour the cooled reduction into a glass bottle—an empty balsamic bottle works well. (The reduction can be stored for up to 3 months, in the refrigerator or pantry. The strained blueberries can be made into a tangy spread that pairs well with cheese.)

Crispy-fried shallots Put rice flour into a shallow bowl. Add shallots and toss to coat.

Heat oil in a deep fryer or deep saucepan to a temperature of 250°F. Gently deep-fry shallots for 6 to 8 minutes, until golden brown. Using a slotted spoon, transfer shallots to a paper towel–lined plate. Season with salt. Set aside.

Peach salad In a bowl, stir peaches with Tajin and salt. Arrange peaches in the center of a serving plate. Drizzle blueberry-balsamic reduction over and around the peaches.

In the same bowl, combine herbs and jalapeño and scatter on top of the peaches. Scatter feta on top and garnish with crispy-fried shallots. Finish with lemon juice.

Note: Tajin is a Mexican seasoning mix made with chiles, sea salt, and dehydrated lime juice. It can be purchased at spice shops and at Fiesta or other major supermarkets.

Helen Greek Food and Wine

WILLIAM WRIGHT

★ With the charm of a contemporary Greek taverna, Helen Greek in Rice Village is rustic modern with its high ceilings, exposed-brick walls, and oversized mounted mirrors. The long space is stylishly divided into dining room and bar by a wine gantry—stocked with an alluring selection of Greek wines.

Chef William Wright nails the flavors of Greek cuisine as if he were born on an island in the Ionian Sea, but the food at Helen Greek is not at all stereotypical. While the dishes bring a regional taste of Greece, Wright embraces seasonality with local ingredients. For instance, the seasonal fried squash flowers are paired with an original creamy skordalia (page 120), and the gyros is made with marinated Black Hill Ranch pork roasted on the vertical spit.

Wright was an anthropology major before his passion for food took him to culinary school in New York first, and then in Italy. His avid interest in cultures compelled him to study original recipes and discover what made one region inherently different from another. He translates his research into exquisite dishes such as the Cretan *gamopilafo*, a risotto-like dish using tender, braised lamb shank, and rabbit steeped in wild Greek mountain tea and served with a caramelized fennel and lemon vinaigrette.

In 2017, Helen Greek opened a second location in the Heights—with one of the coziest patios in town, covered and relaxed. And the menus vary enough between the two restaurants that one could easily visit both in the same week and end up eating different Greek food altogether: enjoying the culinary focus on a specific Greek region at Rice Village, or eating your way through a tempting list of mezze and classics like *pastitsio* (Greece's version of baked pasta) and *stifado* (stewed lamb) in the Heights.

▶ **Beet Salad with Avocado-Yogurt Dressing** | p. 118–19

Grilled marinated olives

2½ cups Halkidiki olives, pitted and rinsed

½ cup olive oil, plus extra as needed

2 large cloves garlic, thinly sliced

2½ Tbsp coriander seeds, crushed

2½ Tbsp chopped cilantro leaves and a little stem

Dried citrus

1 lemon, unpeeled

1 orange, unpeeled

1 small red ruby grapefruit, unpeeled

Roasted beets

4 beets, peeled and cut into 8 wedges

4 sprigs thyme

1 clove garlic

1 bay leaf

1 tsp kosher salt

1 tsp black pepper

1 cup vegetable stock

½ cup white wine

Beet purée

2 cups Roasted Beets (see here)

1 clove roasted garlic (see here)

3 to 4 green olives, pitted

1 Tbsp capers, drained

1 tsp finely chopped basil

1 tsp finely chopped mint

½ to 1 cup extra-virgin olive oil

⅓ cup reserved Roasted Beets juice (see here)

Salt and black pepper

Beet Salad with Avocado-Yogurt Dressing

SERVES 4 TO 6 This ravishing beet salad may have a lot of components but don't let that deter you: they're simple to prepare and super versatile. Add chicken stock to leftover beet purée and you have soup; the mellow and creamy avocado-yogurt dressing is fabulous with roasted chicken; and the dried citrus and marinated olives are the perfect cocktail garnish.

Grilled marinated olives Pat dry the olives between layers of paper towel. Skewer 10 to 12 olives through the side. (Use flat 10-inch metal skewers, so the olives stay in place when you flip them over.)

Preheat a grill over high heat. Grill skewered olives for 45 seconds on each side or until grill marks are visible. (Turn only once.) Transfer olives to a plate to cool, then remove from the skewers and put them into a heatproof bowl.

Heat oil in a small saucepan over medium heat. Add garlic and coriander seeds and gently simmer for 1 to 2 minutes. Carefully pour the hot oil over the charred olives, add cilantro and stir to mix.

Pour olives into a clean and dry jar, topping up with more oil as needed to keep the olives submerged. Cover and refrigerate for at least 24 hours and up to 1 week for better infusion.

Dried citrus Preheat oven to 200°F.

Cut the lemon, orange, and grapefruit into ⅛-inch-thick wheels. Place them in a single layer on a baking sheet and dry in the oven for 2 to 4 hours, until the citrus are dry to the touch and snap when you try to fold them. Set aside.

Roasted beets Preheat oven to 400°F.

Place beets in an ovenproof casserole, add the remaining ingredients, stirring to mix, and cover with foil. Roast for 30 minutes or until beets are tender.

Strain the liquid into a bowl. Measure out 2 cups beets and set the remaining beets aside. Reserve the clove garlic.

Beet purée Purée all ingredients in a blender until smooth.

Charred scallions

4 to 6 scallions, roots trimmed

1 Tbsp olive oil

Salt and black pepper

Avocado-yogurt dressing

1 ripe avocado

1 clove garlic, chopped

2 Tbsp white wine vinegar

1 tsp dried or fresh dill

¼ cup + 3 Tbsp plain full-fat yogurt

¼ cup extra-virgin olive oil

1 tsp Aleppo pepper

Salt

Sesame seasoning

¼ cup sesame seeds

1 Tbsp dried mint

½ Tbsp Aleppo pepper

1 dried orange slice (see here), crumbled

1 tsp sea salt, or to taste

Assembly

4 to 6 handfuls mixed greens, radicchio (torn), and arugula

2 Tbsp Avocado-Yogurt Dressing (see here)

Salt and black pepper

Roasted Beets (see here)

2 Tbsp Sesame Seasoning (see here)

2 cups Beet Purée (see here)

Charred Scallions (see here)

Grilled marinated olives

Dried Citrus (see here)

Charred scallions Preheat a grill over high heat. Brush scallions with oil and grill for 1 minute on each side or until lightly charred. (Alternatively, char them in a frying pan over high heat.) Transfer scallions to a chopping board and coarsely chop. Put them into a bowl and season with salt and pepper. Set aside.

Avocado-yogurt dressing In a blender, purée avocado, garlic, vinegar, dill, ¼ cup yogurt, and oil for 30 seconds until smooth. Pour into a bowl. Using a small spatula or spoon, mix in the remaining 3 tablespoons yogurt and Aleppo pepper. Season with salt.

Sesame seasoning Heat a small frying pan for 30 seconds over high heat. Toast sesame seeds, shaking the pan regularly, for 1 minute or until golden brown. Pour into a bowl and add mint, Aleppo pepper, dried orange, and salt.

Assembly Put greens into a bowl and dress with avocado-yogurt dressing. Season with salt and pepper. Put the roasted beet wedges into a separate bowl and toss with sesame seasoning.

Arrange beets on individual plates and pipe beet purée in between. Top with greens, scallions, and marinated olives. Finish with the citrus (whole for dramatic presentation, or you can scatter broken-up pieces).

Note: Leftover dried citrus can be eaten as snacks, crumbled and made into citrus sugar, or added to marinades. And they make for great (edible) decorations and cocktail garnishes.

Stuffed blossoms

12 to 15 zucchini blossoms
1 cup ricotta
1 tsp dried thyme
1 tsp dried oregano
1 tsp grated lemon zest
1 tsp salt, or to taste

Batter

½ cup chickpea flour
½ cup rice flour
2 tsp baking powder
1 tsp salt
1 tsp black pepper
1 tsp olive oil
¼ cup ouzo or other anise liqueur (optional)

1 cup grated mizithra, ricotta salata, or Parmesan
1½ cups ice-cold sparkling water

Roasted garlic paste

1 head garlic
½ Tbsp olive oil

Stuffed Zucchini Blossoms with Skordalia

SERVES 4 TO 5 If you need an inspired recipe to fill those bright yellow, fresh zucchini blossoms you found at the market, look no further. This crafty recipe has the blossoms coated in chickpea batter, making it an ideal gluten-free option. The skordalia, a Greek garlic spread, also makes for a delightful dip for warm pita or accompanying sauce for grilled fish.

Stuffed blossoms Using tweezers, gently open the blossoms and remove the yellow pollen-covered stamens. Set the blossoms aside.

In a bowl, combine ricotta, herbs, zest, and salt and mix well. Spoon the mixture into a piping bag. (Alternatively, put it into a sealable bag and cut off one of the bottom corners of the bag.)

Gently open a blossom and fill it with ½ tablespoon filling. Fold over the petals and transfer to a plate. Repeat with the remaining blossoms.

Batter Sift both flours into a mixing bowl. Add baking powder, salt, pepper, oil, and liqueur, if using. Stir in cheese.

Pour in ½ cup ice-cold sparkling water and mix well. Add the rest of the sparkling water in a steady stream, stirring until mixture is the consistency of a thin pancake batter.

Roasted garlic paste Preheat oven to 400°F.

Cut the top off the head of garlic, then place garlic on a piece of foil large enough to wrap it. Drizzle oil over the garlic and wrap in the foil. Roast for 30 minutes or until softened and browned. Unwrap and let cool.

Squeeze out the garlic cloves and transfer to a bowl. Using a spoon, mash the cloves into a paste and set aside.

Skordalia In a small food processor, process garlic, oil, vinegar, garlic paste, honey, and salt on medium-high speed until a runny paste is formed. Add walnuts and pulse for 2 minutes or until mixture turns thick and smooth. Add parsley and process for another 30 seconds to incorporate.

Transfer to a small serving bowl, drizzle with honey, and garnish with mint and salt flakes.

Skordalia

- 1 clove garlic, finely chopped
- ½ cup extra-virgin olive oil
- ⅓ cup white wine vinegar
- 2 Tbsp Roasted Garlic Paste (see here)
- 2 Tbsp honey, plus extra for drizzling
- 2 tsp salt, or to taste
- 2 cups toasted walnuts
- 5 Tbsp chopped Italian parsley
- Mint leaves, for garnish
- Flaky sea salt, for finishing

Assembly

- Vegetable oil, for deep-frying
- ¼ cup cornstarch or rice flour, plus extra as needed, for coating

Assembly Heat oil in a deep fryer or deep saucepan to a temperature of 350°F.

Do a test by dipping 1 zucchini blossom in the batter to see how it sticks. If the batter doesn't coat the blossom well (the blossom needs to be absolutely dry), dust each blossom with ½ teaspoon cornstarch (or rice flour) before dipping in the batter.

Dip the zucchini blossoms in batter, then carefully lower 4 to 5 blossoms into the oil. (Work in batches to avoid overcrowding.) Deep-fry for 6 to 8 minutes, until blossoms are crisp, golden, and float to the surface. Remove with a slotted spoon and drain on a paper towel–lined plate. Repeat with the remaining blossoms.

Serve hot with skordalia on the side.

Himalaya Restaurant and Catering

KAISER LASHKARI

★ Himalaya may seem like an unassuming eatery in Little India, but this mom-and-pop is a Houston institution. It is a distinction that comes from serving stellar Indian-Pakistani food since 2004. Karachi-born owner Kaiser Lashkari and his wife, Azra, have cooked their way into the hearts of many a loyal client, including several Houston chefs who swing by on days off to tuck into succulent kebabs, aromatic curries, char-bubbled naan, and the fluffiest of biryanis. Beyond local fans, Himalaya garnered national attention after appearances on Andrew Zimmern's *Bizarre Foods* and in the Houston episode of the late Anthony Bourdain's *Parts Unknown*.

Lashkari, who immigrated to the U.S. nearly forty years ago, dropped out of medical school to pursue his passion for cooking. In 1986, he graduated with a master's in hotel and restaurant management from Hilton College and began working in hotel restaurants around the city. In 1992, he opened a takeout and catering company, his dream of opening a restaurant eventually coming true in 2004 with Himalaya.

Lashkari cooks all morning—toasting and grinding spices, leavening bread doughs, marinating meats, and simmering curries—before becoming an amiable and gracious host in the dining room for lunch and dinner. Himalaya will satisfy cravings for authentic Pakistani dishes such as chicken *achaari* (pickle-spiced curry) and a Peshawari beef stew called *gosht karhai*, but Lashkari also shows off his vegetable-forward Indian repertoire with treasured dishes like mild-curried eggplant, buttery vegetable dumplings, and okra masala.

Houston flavors make their way into the menu in what he calls "friendly fusions." His flaky paratha, cooked quesadilla-style (the "paratha-dilla"), and the very popular Himalaya fried chicken (HFC) are already Houston staples. It's the kind of food that comes from a chef who enjoys connecting with his guests, and it earned him a James Beard nomination for Best Chef Southwest.

2 lbs flaky white fish

¼ cup vegetable or peanut oil (divided)

2 yellow onions, finely chopped

1 cup mashed potatoes

6 green chiles, seeded and finely chopped

2 bunches cilantro, finely chopped

4 large cloves garlic, finely chopped

1¼ tsp ground cumin

1 tsp red chili powder (Indian)

½ tsp ground turmeric

4 large eggs, beaten well (divided)

Salt

2 cups panko breadcrumbs

Chopped Italian parsley, for garnish

Cherry tomatoes, halved, for garnish

Sweet-and-sour tamarind chutney, to serve (optional)

Spicy Fish Cakes

SERVES 4 TO 6 These crispy-fried fish cakes, with their chile kick and refreshing herbs, make a great snack at any time of day. This is the perfect recipe for using up leftover fish or boiled potatoes. As a meal, Kaiser Lashkari combines them with lentils and rice, or with a vegetable biryani. You can also serve it with steamed rice and sautéed vegetables, for a simple midweek meal.

Bring a saucepan of water to a boil over high heat. Add fish, reduce heat to low, and cook for 2 minutes or until flaky. Using a slotted spoon, transfer fish to a paper towel–lined plate to drain.

Heat 1 tablespoon oil in a frying pan over medium heat. Add onions and cook for 2 to 3 minutes, until softened. Set aside to cool.

In a large bowl, combine fish, onions, potatoes, chiles, cilantro, garlic, spices, and half the eggs and, using your hands, mix well. Season with salt.

Using a ½-cup measure, portion out mixture, shaping each portion into round patties about ½ inch thick. Set aside on a wax paper–lined baking sheet.

Prepare two bowls: one with the remaining beaten egg and one with panko. Dip each fish cake in egg, then dredge in panko to coat. Set aside on the prepared baking sheet.

Heat 2 to 3 tablespoons oil in a frying pan (enough to create a shallow layer) over medium-high heat. Drop in a few panko crumbs; if they sizzle right away, the oil is hot enough. Add a few fish cakes and cook for 35 to 40 seconds on each side, until golden and crisp. Transfer to a paper towel–lined plate. Repeat with the remaining fish cakes.

Arrange on a platter and garnish with parsley and tomatoes. Serve immediately with tamarind chutney, if using, on the side.

Indian fried onions

3 cups canola oil, for deep-frying

4 large white onions, thinly sliced from root to top

Green shrimp curry

6 serrano peppers, stemmed and seeded

2 bunches cilantro

¾ cup coconut milk powder

¼ cup Fried Onions (see here)

1 tsp cumin seeds

1 tsp salt

¼ cup white vinegar

2 Tbsp vegetable oil

2 lbs large shrimp, peeled and deveined

Brown lamb curry

8 dried red chiles

1 knob ginger, peeled and grated

2 to 3 large cloves garlic, crushed

½ cup Fried Onions (see here)

1¼ tsp ground cumin

1 tsp ground coriander

1 tsp ground turmeric

2 Tbsp vegetable oil (divided)

2 Tbsp lemon juice

1½ lbs lean ground lamb

½ cup tomato paste

1 tsp garam masala

Kaiser's Rainbow Rice

SERVES 10 TO 12 Kaiser Lashkari's rainbow rice is a feast of flavor and color, a medley of green shrimp curry, seasoned lamb, and tomato-red chicken running through basmati rice. The dish is then finished with fried onions, cilantro, lemon wedges, and eggs. A chef favorite, it's special enough to be the pièce de résistance at the best dinner parties.

Indian fried onions Heat oil in a wok or deep frying pan over high heat. To check if the oil is hot, add a piece of onion to the oil. If it fries up, add the rest.

Using a long-handled fork, stir onions to separate. Reduce heat to medium-high and fry for 5 minutes, stirring every 2 minutes, until browned. Using a slotted spoon, transfer onions to a paper towel–lined baking sheet and spread out. Leave them to cool in a single layer for 10 minutes or until dry and crispy. Set aside.

Green shrimp curry Place all ingredients except oil and shrimp in a blender. Blend, adding enough cold water to form a thick paste.

Heat oil in a large frying pan over low heat. Add paste and cook for 5 minutes. Add shrimp and sauté for another 3 minutes or until just cooked through. Set aside.

Brown lamb curry In a blender, blend chiles, ginger, garlic, fried onions, spices, 1 tablespoon oil, and lemon juice to form a thick paste.

Heat the remaining 1 tablespoon oil in a large frying pan over medium-high heat. Add paste and cook for 3 to 4 minutes. Add lamb and tomato paste, reduce heat to low, and cook for 12 to 15 minutes. Stir in garam masala. Set aside.

Red chicken curry

- 1 (14.5-oz) can diced tomatoes
- ¼ cup tomato paste
- ½ cup Fried Onions (see here)
- ⅓ cup apple cider vinegar
- ¼ cup brown sugar
- 2 cloves garlic, finely chopped
- 2 Tbsp full-fat plain yogurt
- 2 Tbsp Madras curry powder
- 1 Tbsp grated ginger
- 1 tsp ground paprika
- 1 tsp ground chili
- 1½ lbs chicken breast, cut into ½-inch cubes

White rice and saffron

- 3 cups extra-long-grain basmati rice (see Note), rinsed well
- 2 Tbsp vegetable oil
- 1 tsp salt
- Few drops of white vinegar
- Pinch of saffron
- ¼ cup warm whole milk

Assembly

- ½ cup Fried Onions (see here)
- ½ bunch cilantro
- 4 to 6 lemon wedges
- 6 large hard-boiled eggs, halved (optional)

Red chicken curry In a bowl, combine all ingredients except chicken.

Heat a large frying pan over medium heat. Pour mixture into the pan, reduce heat to medium-low, and cook for 10 to 15 minutes, until thickened and fragrant. Add chicken, increase heat to medium-high, and cook for 10 to 15 minutes, until the liquid is reduced and thickened to a paste-like consistency.

White rice and saffron Soak rice in a bowl of water for 1 hour. (Soaking the basmati rice yields a softer elongated grain and a shortened cooking time.) Drain.

Fill a large saucepan with water and add oil and salt. Bring to a boil over high heat, then add soaked rice and vinegar. (This prevents the rice from sticking together.) Bring back to a boil, then reduce heat to low, cover, and cook for 8 to 10 minutes, until rice is tender but not mushy. Drain and set aside.

In a small frying pan, dry-roast saffron over high heat for 30 seconds. Transfer to a mortar and pound for 1 to 2 seconds with a pestle. Add milk and steep for 5 minutes.

Put two-thirds of the rice into one bowl and the remaining third into a separate bowl. To the bowl with a third, pour in the saffron milk and stir, to make yellow rice.

Assembly Spread a layer of lamb curry on the bottom of a large, decorative bowl. Top with a layer of white rice, followed by a layer of shrimp curry. Add a layer of white rice, then a layer of chicken curry. Finish with yellow rice and garnish with fried onions, cilantro, lemon wedges, and eggs, if using.

Encourage your guests to dig the serving spoon all the way to the bottom of the bowl and scoop up a spoonful of all layers.

> **Note:** Leftover rainbow rice, layered in an ovenproof bowl, reheats well in the oven the next day. Preheat oven to 350°F, cover rice with foil, and heat for 15 to 20 minutes, until warmed through.

Kaiser's Rainbow Rice | p. 128–29

Izakaya

JEAN-PHILIPPE GASTON

★ Izakaya in Midtown is billed as a modern Japanese gastropub. With a bold black and red interior adorned with paper lanterns and Japanese wall murals, the scene is set. Add to that a head-spinning variety of Japanese whiskey and a menu that includes grilled octopus balls (*takoyaki*), crispy chicken skin skewers (*tori kawa*), karaage, and yakisoba, and the plot thickens. But the menu is anything but predictable.

Chef Jean-Philippe Gaston has a global culinary curiosity, and his menu evolves with it. Gaston, who opened the first raw bar in Houston (the now defunct Cove), isn't afraid to tackle something new and make it his own. From Korean *bulgogi* beef wraps to Hawaiian poke bowls to his whimsical snapper sashimi with charred grapes and pistachio gremolata (page 131), Gaston's dishes are influenced by many cultures. "What some call 'fusion' is how I always ate," he shares. "I grew up with Asian, Latin, and French influences, and I've always combined them."

Once Gaston mastered his Taiwanese dumpling–making skills, he took the dumplings to another level, filling them with quail or venison. He even filled dumplings with duck *carnitas*.

Izakaya's extensive ramen menu boasts more than fourteen types of ramen, including traditional tonkotsu, miso, and shoyu ramen. Adventurous diners will be drawn to the contemporary variations, such as Gaston's bold Mexican-inspired Menoodle Ramen (page 130), or the smooth and creamy foie gras and garlic velouté ramen that pays homage to his French heritage. One thing's for sure, Gaston's global style brings international flair to Izakaya.

▶ **Menoodle Ramen** | p. 130

Ramen stock

1 Tbsp vegetable oil

1 large yellow onion, chopped

1 large carrot, chopped

2 stalks celery, chopped

4 lbs pork trotters

3 (2-oz) packages concentrated pork stock

Adobo

8 guajillo chiles, stemmed and seeded

5 chiles de árbol, stemmed and seeded

1 yellow onion, roughly chopped

3 cloves garlic, crushed

Juice of 1 lime

Juice of 1 orange

1 to 2 cups chicken stock

Salt

Assembly

½ cup Adobo, plus extra to taste (see here)

6 to 8 cups Ramen Stock (see here)

2 cups cooked chickpeas

2 cups chopped reserved pork skin (see here)

2 large eggs

1 (16-oz) pack ramen noodles

Garnish

1 cup shredded Napa cabbage

1 avocado, chopped

1 white onion, thinly sliced

6 to 8 radishes, thinly sliced

4 to 8 slices jalapeño pepper

½ cup bean sprouts

2 lime wedges

Menoodle Ramen

SERVES 4 This dish is a culinary play on ramen noodles and *menudo*, a traditional Mexican beef tripe soup. Instead of tripe, chef Jean-Philippe Gaston combines adobo flavors with gelatinous, collagen-rich pork trotters, which have a similar texture. As pork ramen stock requires all-day tending, pork ramen concentrate is a great alternative; it can be found in Japanese supermarkets or purchased online.

Ramen stock Heat oil in a stockpot over medium-high heat. Add onion, carrot, and celery and sauté for 5 minutes. Add trotters and 3 quarts water and bring to a boil. Reduce heat to low and simmer for 6 to 8 hours, until the meat is falling off the bone. (The trotters should be fully submerged at all times. If necessary, add more water.) Using a slotted spoon, remove trotters and let cool.

Strain stock into another saucepan. Add concentrated pork stock while ramen stock is still hot and set aside. Remove meat from the bones, reserving the skin. (Makes 3 quarts.)

You now have ready-made ramen-style stock at your fingertips! (Leftover stock can be stored in an airtight container in the freezer for up to 3 months.)

Adobo In a stockpot, combine chiles, onion, garlic, lime and orange juice, and enough chicken stock to just cover the chiles. Bring to a boil, then reduce heat to medium-low and simmer for 45 minutes. Strain cooking liquid into a large pot or bowl.

Transfer strained solids to a blender and blend on medium speed. Gradually add in cooking liquid, 1 cup at the time, until mixture forms a thick paste. Season with salt. (Leftover adobo can be stored in the refrigerator for up to 2 months. Use it as a marinade for beef or chicken, or add to beef chili.)

Assembly In a saucepan, combine adobo and stock to make adobo broth. (Add more adobo for a more intense taste.) Add chickpeas and pork skin and bring to a boil.

Bring a small saucepan of water to a boil. Add eggs and cook for 5 to 6 minutes. Drain, then transfer eggs to a bowl of ice water to cool. Peel and halve lengthwise. Set aside.

Bring a large saucepan of water to a boil, add noodles, and cook according to the package directions. Drain and divide between four bowls. Using a slotted spoon, transfer chickpeas and pork meat (including skin) to the bowls. Ladle hot adobo broth over the noodles. Top with egg and garnishes.

Dried lemon zest

4 large lemons

Charred grapes

5 seedless red grapes, halved lengthwise

1 Tbsp lime juice

1 Tbsp extra-virgin olive oil

Pinch of salt

Pistachio gremolata

1 cup shelled pistachios

¼ cup Dried Lemon Zest (see here)

¼ cup dried parsley

½ Tbsp black pepper, plus extra to taste

½ tsp salt

Sashimi

6 oz sashimi-grade snapper

Juice of 1 lime

Sea salt

½ cup Pistachio Gremolata (see here)

Extra-virgin olive oil, for drizzling

Snapper Sashimi with Charred Grapes and Pistachio Gremolata

SERVES 2 You'll love this elegant crudo paired with sweet-fruity grapes and a lemony, nutty crush of gremolata. Pistachio gremolata adds a little oomph to everything, from grilled steak to roasted cauliflower. Instructions are provided for the dried lemon zest, but if you're pressed for time, you can use crushed dry lemons, found in the spice section of Middle Eastern grocery stores.

Dried lemon zest Preheat oven to 200°F. Line a baking sheet with parchment paper.

Grate lemons onto the prepared baking sheet. Bake zest for 20 to 30 minutes, until it easily crumbles between your fingers.

Charred grapes Heat a frying pan over high heat. Cook grapes, flesh-side down, for 1 minute or until caramelized and crunchy. (They should make a squealing sound and start to bounce.) Transfer grapes to a bowl and add lime juice, oil, and salt. Toss gently, then set aside.

Pistachio gremolata Using a pestle and mortar, pound pistachios until coarsely ground.

In a bowl, combine all ingredients. Set aside. (Leftover gremolata can be stored in an airtight jar for up to 3 months.)

Sashimi Placing your knife at a 45-degree angle against the fillet, slice the fish against the grain, about ⅛ inch thick. Wrap a slice of fish around the tip of your thumb to make a floret. Repeat with the remaining slices and arrange them in a row on a serving plate. Lightly drizzle lime juice over the fish and season with salt.

Generously sprinkle pistachio gremolata over the fish. Arrange grapes around the fish. Drizzle oil over and around fish and serve immediately.

LMN hospitality

BRANDI KEY AND JORGE VALENCIA

★ When three friends bundle decades of restaurant experience and a healthy dose of Southern hospitality, good things come to the table. Brandi Key, Jorge Valencia, and Kelly Laudadio started LMN hospitality in 2018, naming the company after their grandmothers—Lola, Martha, and Norene—who taught them the beauty of taking care of others. In fact, their convivial Sunday Supper events prompted them to launch LMN, a company that offers private dining, catering, pop-up events, and restaurant consultancy.

With twenty years of culinary experience in Houston's dining scene, Key has a deft ability to create menus, organize teams, and open new concepts. Key is used to juggling a lot and, in fact, she craves doing so. "I love the shuffle of the multiple concepts and the different food styles," she says. Well versed in global cuisines, Key can just as easily create a perfectly composed dish of garden peas and citrus gnocchi as she can break down a whole hog and conjure up five unique dishes (as she did for Cochon555's culinary heritage-breed pork competition).

Cooking alongside his grandmother and father in Mexico, Valencia realized his talents early on and often experimented in his home kitchen. He cut his teeth at (now closed) Arcodoro, and dedicated more than twenty-five years to the hospitality industry, both front and back of house, but the kitchen is where he is happiest.

Valencia and Key in the kitchen together is a recipe for success. And with Laudadio playing "ringmaster"—the hostess oversees all marketing and planning—the three friends have every aspect of the food biz covered, from soup to nuts.

▸ **Poblano and Corn Soup with Lobster "Chorizo" and Lime Crema** | p. 134–35
and Crispy Pork and Yucca with Slaw | p. 137

Poblano soup

6 ears corn

4 poblano peppers

3 Tbsp butter

¾ tsp kosher salt,
  plus extra to taste

1 cup cold chicken stock

1 cup heavy cream

½ tsp black pepper,
  plus extra to taste

1 tsp white vinegar

4 thin slices jalapeño
  pepper, for garnish

4 small cilantro leaves,
  for garnish

Poblano and Corn Soup with Lobster "Chorizo" and Lime Crema

SERVES 4 Mild, earthy-fresh poblano peppers are the perfect partner for sweet corn in chef Jorge Valencia's decadent soup. While the verdant green soup tastes great on its own, the addition of smoked chile–brushed lobster and lime crema make it a home run. And if you're itching to add a pinch of smoky ancho to the soup, go right ahead. We won't stop you.

Poblano soup Remove the husks from the corn, place a corn ear upright on a cutting board, and scrape off the kernels with a sharp knife. Repeat for the remaining corn ears.

Char the whole poblano peppers over an open flame on a gas stovetop or under a broiler for 6 to 8 minutes, until the skin is completely blackened. Transfer peppers to a plastic bag and let sit for 10 minutes to loosen the skin. When cool enough to handle, remove skin, stem, and seeds (do not rinse under the tap). Cut the peppers into ½-inch pieces and set aside.

Heat butter in a sauté pan over medium-low heat until it just begins to melt. Add corn and sweat for 10 minutes or until corn is tender. Add salt and sweat for another 5 minutes. Remove from heat and set aside.

In a blender, process roasted peppers, corn, and stock until smooth. Pass through a fine-mesh strainer into a saucepan. Set saucepan over medium-high heat and bring mixture to a simmer. Add cream and simmer for 10 minutes or until slightly reduced. Add pepper and vinegar and simmer for another 10 minutes. Season with more salt and pepper.

Lobster

4 (5-oz) lobster tail
¼ tsp chipotle powder
¼ tsp ancho powder
¼ tsp kosher salt
¼ tsp black pepper
2 Tbsp butter
1 Tbsp extra-virgin
   olive oil
2 cloves garlic, finely
   chopped

Crema

3 Tbsp sour cream
1 Tbsp + 1 tsp lime juice
¼ tsp kosher salt
¼ tsp black pepper

Lobster Remove the lobster meat from the shell and chop into ⅛- to ¼-inch pieces. Add chipotle and ancho powders, salt, and pepper to the lobster meat and mix well.

Combine butter, oil, and garlic in a small saucepan over medium heat and heat until oil begins to bubble. Add lobster meat and cook for 3 minutes or until the lobster is just cooked through. Remove the lobster from the seasoned oil and set both aside.

Crema In a small bowl, mix all ingredients and ½ tablespoon water until smooth and runny enough to drizzle over the soup.

Assembly Ladle the soup into individual serving bowls. Place a spoonful of the lobster in the middle of the soup. Drizzle lime crema in an abstract pattern on top. Dot the seasoned oil on the soup. Garnish with a thin slice of jalapeño and a small cilantro leaf.

Pork and yucca

- 2 (12-oz) packages salt pork, rinsed
- 1 large yucca, peeled and cut into 1-inch cubes
- 1 white onion, chopped
- 1 head garlic, top removed to expose the cloves
- 4 bay leaves
- 1 tsp chili flakes
- 4 cups chicken stock
- 3 cups vegetable oil

Slaw

- ½ green cabbage, thinly shaved
- ½ white onion, thinly sliced
- ½ jicama, peeled and cut into ⅛- × 2-inch strips
- 3 radishes, cut into ⅛-inch strips
- 1 Asian pear, peeled, cored, and quartered, then cut into ⅛- × 2-inch strips
- 1 Tbsp extra-virgin olive oil
- Juice of 1 lime
- 1 tsp kosher salt
- ½ tsp black pepper

Assembly

- ½ bunch cilantro, leaves only, for garnish
- 2 scallions, chopped, for garnish
- ½ Tbsp chili oil
- ¼ tsp chili flakes
- 4 lime wedges

Crispy Pork and Yucca with Slaw

SERVES 4 Chef Brandi Key's recipe is a tasty tango between salted pork belly and yucca, complemented by a lively slaw of crisp jicama and fruity Asian pear. It brightens up your morning, or provides an energizing bite for lunch. Take care when frying the cooked pork and yucca cubes: although frying allows them to crisp up beautifully, they may splatter! For the slaw, Key recommends using a mandolin to cut the vegetables into uniform strips.

Pork and yucca Using a sharp knife, score the salt pork skin in a crosshatch pattern, evenly spacing the scores 1 inch apart and making long slits through the skin but not into the meat. Cut the salt pork into ½-inch cubes.

Place pork in a saucepan and cover with cold water. Bring to a boil over high heat, then remove from heat and drain. Return pork to the saucepan and repeat this process two more times. (The process removes excess salt and helps tenderize the meat.)

Return pork to the saucepan, add yucca, onion, garlic head, bay leaves, and chili flakes. Pour in enough stock just to cover and bring to a boil over high heat. Reduce heat to medium-low and simmer for 12 to 15 minutes, until yucca is tender when pierced with a fork. Drain mixture and transfer to a paper towel–lined baking sheet to dry for at least 5 minutes. Remove the garlic head and set aside to cool. Discard bay leaves.

Squeeze out the garlic cloves from the head, keeping the cloves intact. Set aside.

Heat oil in a large, deep-frying pan over medium heat for 5 minutes. Working in batches, if necessary, add pork mixture in a single layer, taking care to not splatter the oil. Fry for 10 minutes, stirring occasionally, or until yucca and pork are golden and tender. Add garlic and cook for another 10 minutes or until pork and yucca are crispy. Using a slotted spoon, transfer the mixture to a paper towel–lined plate.

Slaw Stir together all ingredients to mix well. Adjust seasoning to taste.

Assembly Transfer slaw to a large serving platter. Arrange pork and yucca on top and around the slaw. Garnish with cilantro and scallions and finish with chili oil, chili flakes, and lime wedges.

Maison Degaine / MONA

SIDNEY DEGAINE

★ Born and raised on the Côte d'Azur, chef Sidney Degaine is bound to have French classics like ratatouille, bouillabaisse, and *soupe au pistou* in his culinary DNA. After graduating from the prestigious Lycée Paul Augier in France, Degaine worked with Alain Ducasse at Le Louis XV in Monaco and went on to become the executive chef for the French national soccer team during the 2014 World Cup. He headed the kitchen at the Sun Valley Resort in Idaho and then moved to Brazil, where he and his wife ran three restaurants before they settled in Houston and opened Café Azur in 2016.

With rave reviews and busy nights, Degaine carved his name on the Houston food scene with dishes such as the "perfect egg" in potato foam (page 139), duck confit drizzled with orange glaze, and his bouillabaisse. In spite of the success with Café Azur, Degaine felt restricted by the confines of a fine-dining restaurant and was ready for a different concept, one where good food made with farm-fresh ingredients could be accessed by a much wider audience. In 2018, Degaine launched MONA, an Italian food counter-service restaurant. With its tomato plants, potted herbs, and endlessly sheets of pasta drying behind the counter, MONA looks and feels like a place where food is made from scratch. "Guests select their own house-made pasta, combine it with farm-to-table ingredients, and have the dishes sautéed in front of them," explains Maria.

In addition to expanding MONA, Degaine continues to cook modern French cuisine as a private chef with Maison Degaine catering. For Sidney, that is the best of both worlds!

Potato mash

1 russet potato, peeled
   and diced small

2 cups heavy cream

Salt

Perfect egg

4 large eggs

1 cup chanterelles or other
   mushrooms, cleaned

Sea salt and black pepper

Assembly

4 cups Potato Mash
   (see here)

White truffle oil

Chives and/or
   microgreens, for
   garnish

½ cup shaved Parmesan

Black pepper

The Perfect Egg

SERVES 4 This elegant dish, served in a slanted glass bowl, first appeared on the menu at Café Azur. The "perfect" egg here refers to an egg cooked at a constant 149°F. You'll need an immersion circulator and a whipped-cream dispenser, but if you're not ready for the modern techniques, we also have a simpler method.

Potato mash Cook potato in lightly salted water for 12 minutes or until it can be easily pierced with a fork. Drain, then mash until smooth. (You can also press the potato through a ricer so it is completely smooth.) Set aside to cool completely.

Slowly pour in cream and whisk until creamy. Season with salt and set aside.

Perfect egg Set an immersion circulator to 149°F in a container filled with water. Gently lower in the eggs and leave them for 35 minutes. (Alternatively, poach the eggs. Bring a saucepan of water to a boil. Add 1 teaspoon each of white vinegar and salt. One by one, break an egg into the water and poach for 3 minutes or until the whites are set and the yolk still runny. Lift out and set aside.)

Heat a nonstick frying pan over medium heat. Pan-sear mushrooms for 5 minutes or until softened. Season with salt and pepper. Transfer to a plate and set aside.

Assembly Select glass bowls about 4 inches in diameter. Transfer potatoes to a whipped-cream dispenser and charge twice with two nitrous oxide chargers. (Alternatively, use a whisk to bring some air into the potato, though it will not be as fluffy.) Fill each bowl with a layer of potato about 3 inches deep. Carefully peel each egg and gently drop onto the potato. (If you poached the eggs, place them on top.)

Spoon mushrooms on top, drizzle with truffle oil, and garnish with chives (and/or microgreens) and shaved Parmesan. Finish with pepper.

Pickled mustard seeds

2 cups white wine

2 cups white vinegar

1 cup granulated sugar

1 cup yellow mustard seeds

Cured salmon

2 cups kosher salt

1 cup granulated sugar

Grated zest of 2 lemons

Grated zest of 1 orange

2 tsp black pepper

1 tsp ground cumin

1 tsp fennel seeds

1 lb fresh skin-on, center-cut piece salmon

Cucumber-yogurt salad

1 English cucumber, peeled and thinly sliced with a mandolin

3 Tbsp kosher salt, plus extra to taste

2 Tbsp Greek yogurt

Black pepper

Assembly

Mint, tarragon, and/or dill, in sprigs and leaves

2 scallions, white part only, thinly sliced

Small lettuce leaves, carrot ribbons, sliced radish, pepitas, and beetroot powder, for garnish (optional)

2 Tbsp Pickled Mustard Seeds (see here)

Extra-virgin olive oil, for drizzling

Cured Salmon and Yogurt-Cucumber Salad

SERVES 4 TO 6 Lox is one of the easiest things to prepare in a kitchen, requiring no more than a few simple, readily available ingredients. The cure has the essentials of salt and sugar, but it's built up with fragrant citrus and fennel seeds. Be sure to only use the freshest sushi-grade salmon, which has been commercially frozen.

Pickled mustard seeds In a saucepan, combine wine, vinegar, and sugar over medium-high heat and stir for 2 minutes or until sugar is dissolved and liquid begins to boil. Turn off heat, then add mustard seeds and cover. Set aside and let steep for 1 hour.

Set aside 2 tablespoons pickled mustard seeds and transfer the remaining mustard seeds to a sterilized jar. Add enough cooking liquid to just cover the mustard seeds. Seal and refrigerate for up to 1 month. (Pickled mustard seeds can be added to a sandwich or a mustard-cream sauce or served with cubes of Old Amsterdam.)

Cured salmon In a mixing bowl, combine salt, sugar, citrus zests, and spices. On a work surface, lay a piece of plastic wrap large enough to wrap the salmon piece twice.

Place ½ cup curing mix in the center of the plastic and lay salmon fillet, skin-side down, on top. Put the remaining curing mix on top and tightly wrap the plastic wrap around the salmon twice. Refrigerate for 24 hours, skin-side down.

Unwrap salmon, wipe off the curing mix, put the salmon into a bowl of cold water, and let sit for 20 minutes.

Remove salmon from the bath and pat dry with paper towel. Cover with paper towel and refrigerate until needed.

Cucumber-yogurt salad Put cucumber into a colander and sprinkle with salt. Let sit for 20 minutes.

Transfer cucumber to a bowl filled with cold water to rinse off salt. Drain, then add yogurt and season with pepper.

Assembly Spoon some cucumber-yogurt salad onto the center of each plate. Thinly slice the salmon and arrange on top of the salad. Garnish with herbs, scallions, and lettuce leaves, carrot, radish, pepitas, and beetroot powder, if using. Add dollops of pickled mustard seeds to each plate. Drizzle with oil and serve.

Mala Sichuan Bistro

CORI XIONG

⭐ Anyone who has dined at Mala Sichuan Bistro has experienced first-hand the numbing sensation of Sichuan peppercorns. In fact, you'll find reference to it even in the restaurant name: *ma* refers to that numbing tingle of Sichuan pepper and *la* means spicy in Chinese. And good *mala* can be enjoyed in this restaurant's dan dan noodles, mapo tofu, and kung pao chicken.

Owner Cori Xiong, born and raised in Chengdu, immigrated to Houston when she was twelve. Her first exposure to American-Chinese cuisine involved General Tso's chicken and fortune cookies—neither of which she knew from growing up in China. Fast-forward to 2011 and Xiong and husband, Heng Chen, open Mala Sichuan Bistro in Chinatown.

At first, they had only Chinese customers. Comparing those early years to building a castle brick by brick, Xiong did every-thing she could to make Sichuanese cuisine accessible to other diners, offering detailed menu descriptions and waiting on tables so she herself could describe the dishes. The restaurant began to receive posi-tive reviews, and non-Chinese customers started coming.

Xiong and her husband eventually opened locations in Montrose, Katy, Sugar Land, and downtown. For Xiong and Chen, it's been an incredible journey seeing Hous-ton's familiarity with Sichuanese cuisine grow, and it's been an incredible journey to see Houstonians develop an apprecia-tion and understanding of Sichuanese and regional Chinese cuisine. "People walk into our restaurant now knowing what they're getting into." At the counter restaurant in the upscale Finn Hall on Main Street, diners routinely stop by for the mapo tofu or kung pao chicken. After all, if your menu reads like a love letter to your cuisine, everybody will want a taste.

Pepper paste	Sichuan rooster	Assembly	
¼ cup green Sichuan peppercorns (see Note)	1 (1½- to 2-lb) fresh young rooster, organic chicken, or guinea hen	Reserved chicken stock (see here)	½ Tbsp sesame oil
1 cup roughly chopped scallion, green parts only	5 scallions, cut into 1-inch pieces, plus extra for garnish	1 (5-inch) piece of lotus root, sliced ⅛ inch thick	1 Tbsp salt
	2 knobs ginger, sliced	¼ cauliflower, florets only	Chopped scallions, for garnish
	5 bay leaves	1 cup sliced cooked bamboo shoots	Fresh herbs such as parsley and/or cilantro, for garnish
	1 star anise	Rooster meat (see here)	
		Pepper paste (see here)	

Sichuan Peppercorn Rooster

SERVES 4 This traditional dish is prepared with fresh young rooster, which tends to be leaner and more flavorful than hen, but feel free to use a young chicken or guinea fowl.

Pepper paste Soak peppercorns in a bowl of warm water for 10 minutes. Drain, then pick off any stems and black seeds.

Using a knife, chop peppercorns and scallions together until they have a pasty texture. (This traditional technique requires some effort and time, but it is worth it. A food processor will make the scallions watery, and the friction and heat of the blade will destroy some of the peppercorn fragrance.) Set aside.

Sichuan rooster Rinse rooster under running water and pat dry with paper towel.

In a stockpot set over medium heat, stir together scallions, ginger, bay leaves, and star anise for 3 minutes, until fragrant. (Be careful to not burn.) Add rooster and enough water to cover it entirely. Bring to a boil over high heat, then reduce heat to medium and simmer for 30 minutes. Using a slotted spoon, skim any foam from the surface. Reduce heat to low and simmer for 10 minutes.

Transfer rooster to a bowl and let cool to room temperature. Once cooled, refrigerate for 40 minutes. Pull meat off bones, leaving the skin (it has a lot of flavor), and coarsely chop. Reserve stock for later use.

Assembly In a saucepan, bring reserved stock to a boil over high heat. Reduce heat to medium and add lotus root and cauliflower florets. Boil for 2 minutes, then add the bamboo shoots and boil for another minute. Strain the vegetables out of the stock and immediately transfer to a bowl of ice water to cool.

In a bowl, mix the meat, strained vegetables, pepper paste (2 tablespoons peppercorn paste for every 2 cups meat), 1 tablespoon of the chicken stock, and sesame oil. Toss gently and season with salt. Plate, garnish with scallions and fresh herbs, and serve.

Note: Sichuan peppercorns are not actually peppercorns but tiny berries that grow on the prickly ash tree and are available as red or green. Green Sichuan peppercorns have a fresh, citrusy taste. Make sure you buy the dried husks and not the whole peppercorns, which would require opening them up and removing the shiny black (and gritty) seed.

Tilapia

1 (1- to 1 ½-lb) whole tilapia, scaled and gutted

1 Tbsp rice cooking wine (preferably Shaoxing)

¼ tsp salt

1 thick slice ginger

1½ scallions, cut into 1-inch pieces

Peanut oil, for deep-frying

½ cup chopped cilantro, for garnish

Steamed rice, to serve

Chili sauce

½ cup canola oil

1 cup dried red chiles

2 Tbsp Sichuan fermented broad bean paste

1 Tbsp red Sichuan peppercorns

5 cloves garlic, thinly sliced

1 thin slice ginger

1 Tbsp rice cooking wine (preferably Shaoxing)

1 Tbsp oyster sauce

2 tsp granulated sugar

¼ tsp sesame oil

1 Tbsp chili flakes

1½ scallions, cut into 1-inch pieces

Note: The dried chiles are used for flavor and to brighten the dish, but the tough-skinned chiles are not meant to be eaten. After serving, you can move them to the side.

Mala Pot-Roasted Tilapia

SERVES 1 TO 2 Owner Cori Xiong is proud of this award-winning recipe from her first chef, Rong Wu. And rightly so: the sauce scintillates with lots of fresh ginger, chile heat, and that teasing tingle of Sichuan pepper. Find all ingredients in supermarkets like 99 Ranch Market or Hong Kong Food Market, where you'll also find a great selection of live fish, including tilapia, sea bream, and pompano.

Tilapia Using a sharp knife, make 4 slashes across the sides of the fish (where the flesh is the thickest). Place fish in a deep dish large enough to hold it.

In a small bowl, combine cooking wine and salt and brush over fish. Place ginger and half the scallions on top of the fish and refrigerate for 30 minutes to marinate. Rinse fish under cold running water, then pat dry.

Heat oil in a large deep fryer to a temperature of 320°F to 350°F. Place fish in the frying basket and carefully lower it into the hot oil. Fry for 2 minutes or until the skin is crisp and golden. Remove the basket from the deep fryer and transfer the fish to a plate.

Chili sauce Arrange all the measured ingredients within easy reach of the stove. Heat a large wok over medium heat until lightly smoking. Pour in oil and heat for 30 seconds. Stir in chiles, broad bean paste, and peppercorns and cook for 1 to 2 minutes, until fragrant and bubbling. Add garlic and ginger and stir for another minute.

Pour in 3 cups hot water and stir. Add cooking wine, oyster sauce, and sugar. Increase heat to high, add the deep-fried fish, and bring to a boil. Reduce heat to medium and simmer, uncovered, for 8 minutes. Using a wide spatula, carefully flip the fish, taking care not to damage it. Simmer for 7 minutes or until the liquid is reduced and fish is cooked through but not breaking apart. Stir in sesame oil.

Transfer fish to a serving platter. Leave sauce in the wok and increase heat to high. Add chili flakes and scallions, and stir for 2 minutes or until fragrant and sauce is reduced.

Plating Remove sauce from heat and pour over plated fish. Garnish fish with cilantro and serve with steamed rice.

Oporto Fooding House & Wine

RICK DI VIRGILIO AND SHIVA PATEL

⭐ There is romance in food, and then there is food romance! He, Portuguese-Italian, opens the wine and food bar Oporto Café in 2006. She, a London-born Indian, is one of his early regulars, charmed by both the place and the chef. Soon, Rick Di Virgilio and Shiva Patel are cooking together and eventually marry. They open an Indian-cuisine-slash-London-pub, Queen Vic, a mile from Oporto Café and a block from their home, and RISHI Hospitality is born.

Evolving from Oporto Café, RISHI consolidated food and wine in a new venture, labeling it a "fooding house"—restaurant, bakery, café, and wine bar all rolled into one.

"Oporto Fooding House & Wine is the capstone on what we built together," says Di Virgilio, stressing that his father—and biggest supporter throughout—is part of that success. They even gutted and remodeled Queen Vic together.

O2, as Di Virgilio likes to call it, opened in 2015 in Midtown with an extensive menu that beckons.

Come for Portuguese classics such as *francesinha* (a decadent grilled ham and cheese), but also for spice-inspired dishes such as lamb meatballs fragrant with preserved lemon and mint, and grilled octopus with peppery potatoes (page 148). Stay for the dessert menu, featuring those crispy custard tarts, *pasteis de nata*. And pair the outstanding selection of Portuguese and Spanish cheeses with a port or Madeira (there's ample choice of both).

RISHI continues to draw inspiration from the spice route to bring food that connects India and Portugal. We can't wait to find out what the next chapter in this love story will bring.

▶ **Grilled Octopus with Shaak Potatoes and Salsa Verde** | p. 148–49 **and Kashmiri Caipirinha** | p. 151

Octopus

½ small carrot, chopped

½ stalk celery, chopped

½ red onion, chopped

1 bay leaf

½ cinnamon stick

1 wine cork (optional)

1 (2- to 3-lb) octopus, cleaned, innards and eyes removed

1 Tbsp olive oil

Sea salt and black pepper

Salsa verde

½ bunch Italian parsley

½ bunch tarragon

½ bunch mint

2 cloves garlic

1 anchovy fillet

1 tsp capers

½ tsp chili flakes

Grated zest of 1 lemon

3 Tbsp olive oil, plus extra as needed

1 Tbsp apple cider vinegar

1 tsp lemon juice

Shaak potatoes

1 tsp black mustard seeds

2 Tbsp clarified butter (ghee)

½ yellow onion, finely chopped

1 clove garlic, finely chopped

1 tsp grated ginger

½ tsp finely chopped serrano pepper

5 to 6 neem leaves (optional; see Note)

1 tsp ground coriander

½ tsp ground cumin

½ tsp ground turmeric

4 cups vegetable oil, for deep-frying

4 Yukon Gold potatoes, cut into ½-inch cubes

Salt

Grilled Octopus with Shaak Potatoes and Salsa Verde

SERVES 4 A popular item on the menu, this cross-cultural dish teams Portuguese charred octopus with crispy Indian-spiced potatoes and zesty Italian salsa verde. When steaming octopus, chef Rick Di Virgilio honors the Italian tradition of cork-braising by adding a wine cork or two to the mixture. "It's an old wives' tale, of course," he explains. "But my grandmother did it, and so did my mother." Whether you decide to cork or to not cork, this recipe yields a beautifully tender octopus.

Octopus Bring a large pot of water to a boil. Add carrot, celery, onion, bay leaf, cinnamon, and cork, if using, and gently boil over medium heat for 10 to 15 minutes. Using tongs, carefully lower octopus into the pot, reduce heat to low, and simmer for 30 to 45 minutes, until tender when pierced with a knife. Transfer octopus to a baking sheet and let cool.

Reserve 4 legs. Chop up remaining 4 legs, body, and head into ½-inch pieces. Toss lightly with oil and season with salt and pepper.

Salsa verde In a small food processor, pulse herbs, garlic, anchovy, capers, chili flakes, and lemon zest for 1 minute or until smooth.

With the motor running on medium speed, pour in oil in a steady stream until mixture is the consistency of a thick sauce. Transfer mixture to a bowl and stir in vinegar and lemon juice to taste. (The salsa verde should be easy to drizzle but not too liquid.) Set aside.

Shaak potatoes Heat a large, heavy-bottomed frying pan over medium-high heat. Fry mustard seeds for 30 seconds to 1 minute, until they start to pop. Add clarified butter, onion, garlic, ginger, and serrano pepper. Reduce heat to low and cook for 5 to 8 minutes, until onion begins to brown. Add neem leaves, if using, and cook for 2 minutes. Stir in coriander, cumin, and turmeric and cook for another 2 minutes. Remove from heat.

Heat oil in a deep fryer or deep saucepan to a temperature of 300°F. Pat dry the potatoes with a dish towel. Carefully lower potatoes into the oil and deep-fry for 5 to 6 minutes, until golden. Using a slotted spoon, transfer potatoes to a paper

Assembly

4 reserved octopus legs
  (see here)

2 Tbsp olive oil (divided)

2 cloves garlic, thinly
  sliced

Chopped Octopus
  (see here)

Shaak Potatoes (see here)

1 Tbsp lemon juice

1 Tbsp chopped cilantro

¼ cup Salsa Verde
  (see here)

1 lemon, halved and
  grilled

towel–lined plate to drain. Put potatoes into a bowl, add onion mixture, and toss well. Season with salt, then set aside.

Assembly Heat a large frying pan over high heat. Brush octopus legs with 1 tablespoon olive oil. Sear octopus in the pan for 2 to 3 minutes on each side, until charred.

Heat the remaining 1 tablespoon olive oil in another frying pan over high heat. Add garlic, chopped octopus, and shaak potatoes and sauté for 3 to 5 minutes, until heated through. Add lemon juice, toss well, and remove from heat. Toss with cilantro.

Divide the chopped octopus and shaak potatoes among four plates. Place a spoonful of salsa verde on one side of the potatoes. Top each serving with a charred tentacle and serve immediately with grilled lemons.

> **Note:** Neem leaves add a pleasant bitterness to this dish. They can be found in Indian supermarkets.

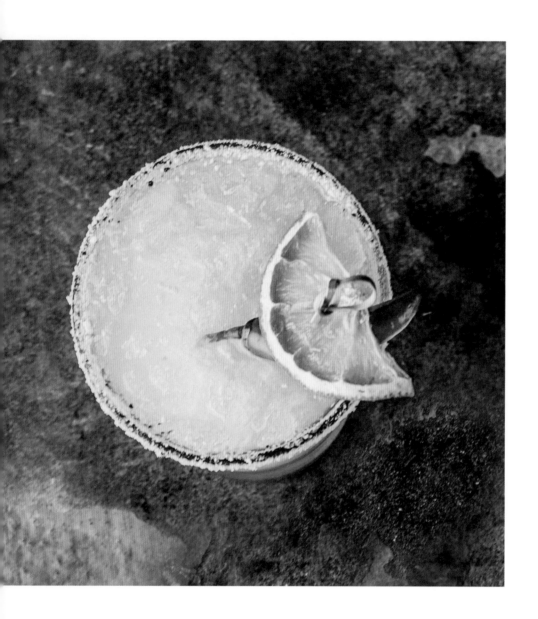

Lemongrass simple syrup

1 cup granulated sugar

1 Tbsp chopped lemongrass

Kashmiri caipirinha

½ Tbsp toasted coconut flakes

½ Tbsp granulated sugar

Dash of ground cardamom

½ oz Lemongrass Simple Syrup (see here)

1 to 2 thin slices serrano pepper

3 thin slices turmeric root

½ oz lime juice

1 bar spoon tamarind concentrate

2 oz good-quality cachaça (preferably Avuá Prata)

1 serrano pepper, for garnish

½ slice dried orange, for garnish

Kashmiri Caipirinha

SERVES 1 The key component of a Caipirinha is cachaça (known as Brazilian rum), distilled from sugar cane juice, and Oporto has an option for every taste—from the classic mix of cachaça, sugar, and lime juice to inventive infusions with curry leaves, green mango powder, and chile heat. Chef-owner (and accomplished bartender) Rick Di Virgilio's Kashmiri Caipirinha is refreshing and bold, with hints of citrusy lemongrass, earthy turmeric, and sour tamarind.

Lemongrass simple syrup In a small saucepan, mix together sugar, lemongrass, and 1 cup water. Bring to a boil and stir for 1 minute to dissolve sugar. Turn off heat and steep for 15 minutes. Strain through a fine-mesh sieve and let cool.

Kashmiri caipirinha Prepare an oversized old-fashioned or stemless wine glass. In a small bowl, mix together coconut flakes, sugar, and cardamom. Wet the rim of the glass with simple syrup and dip it in the coconut mixture.

In a shaker, muddle serrano pepper, turmeric, and lime juice. Add tamarind and cachaça, fill shaker with ice, and shake vigorously for 30 seconds to 1 minute.

Fill the glass halfway with crushed ice. Using a double or fine strainer, pour the cocktail into the prepared glass. Garnish with serrano pepper and orange slice.

The Original Ninfa's on Navigation

ALEX PADILLA

★ At the heart of historic East End, right across from the Esplanade, is The Original Ninfa's on Navigation—or "Ninfa's" for short. The James Beard–nominated restaurant has a formidable reputation for serving up legitimate Tex-Mex food, yet you wouldn't be the first one to drive past the humble low-rise without noticing it. Inside it's a different story, a buzzing hive where meat sizzles on the wood-fired grill, tortillas are rolled and pressed right in front of you, and waiters whisk by you with loaded trays, tickling your nostrils with the aroma of grilled meats, roasted peppers, and melted cheese.

Executive chef Alex Padilla has been creating culinary magic at this Second Ward institution since 2006. The ever-changing menu unites the food traditions of Mexico and Texas: rabbit stewed in guajillo sauce and served with corn tortillas; grilled Texas redfish with chipotle slaw; and *cabrito flautas*, baby goat in corn tortillas, fried crispy. "Tex-Mex is like the perfect marriage," says Padilla. "The flavors blend together really well."

The one item that will never leave the menu is Mama Ninfa's original fajitas. Ninfa's is, after all, where the original owner, Ninfa Laurenzo, first presented soft tortillas wrapped around thinly sliced, well-seasoned grilled skirt steak. She called them *tacos al carbon*, but they became a sensation known as fajitas.

Padilla, whose mother was a line cook in the early days here, compares Ninfa's to an old boat: "It is a classic. Keep it in good shape, and people will say 'Wow, look at that boat!'" And while Ninfa's has expanded with a new Galleria-area location and fast-casual concept, the Original Ninfa's remains a blissful union of Tex and Mex as it has since it opened in 1973.

Coleslaw

½ small green cabbage, cored and shredded

½ red onion, thinly sliced

1 Tbsp extra-virgin olive oil

Juice of ½ lemon

1 tsp finely chopped cilantro

Salt and black pepper

Lemon dressing

1 tsp coriander seeds

½ tsp dried ancho chile seeds (see Note)

¼ cup lemon juice

⅓ cup extra-virgin olive oil

1 tsp apple cider vinegar

¼ tsp dried oregano

3 cloves garlic, finely chopped

Salt and black pepper

Chipotle aioli

½ canned chipotle pepper in adobo sauce, finely chopped

½ cup mayonnaise

1 tsp lemon juice

Salt and black pepper

Octopus tacos

2 bay leaves

¼ cup white vinegar

1 (2-lb) whole octopus, cleaned

2 Tbsp butter

1 clove garlic, finely chopped

Lemon Dressing (see here)

4 flour tortillas, warmed, for serving

Octopus Tacos with Coleslaw and Chipotle Aioli

SERVES 4 Chef Alex Padilla shares the recipe for his popular octopus tacos, a great dish for family dinner fun. Simply put out a spread of coleslaw, chipotle aioli, super-tender octopus, and hot flour tortillas and let everyone build their own tacos.

Coleslaw In a bowl, mix together cabbage and onion.

In a separate bowl, combine oil, lemon juice, and cilantro. Season with salt and pepper. Pour mixture into the bowl of cabbage and mix well to coat. Let sit for 30 minutes.

Lemon dressing Heat a frying pan over high heat. Toast coriander and chile seeds for 1 minute or until they pop. Using a mortar and pestle, pound seeds until coarsely ground.

In a small bowl, combine lemon juice, oil, vinegar, oregano, garlic, and ground spices. Season with salt and pepper, then let sit for at least 30 minutes.

Chipotle aioli In a small bowl, combine chipotle pepper, mayonnaise, and lemon juice. Mix until well incorporated. Season with salt and pepper.

Octopus tacos In a double boiler, combine bay leaves, vinegar, and 4 cups water in the bottom pan and bring to a boil. Place octopus in the top pan and steam for 45 minutes to 1 hour, until tender when gently pierced with a fork.

Transfer octopus to a cutting board and let cool. Chop into 1-inch pieces.

In a small bowl, combine butter and garlic. Heat a large frying pan over medium-high heat. Pour in lemon dressing and cook for 30 seconds to warm through. Add octopus and garlic butter, increase heat to high, and cook for 2 to 3 minutes.

Transfer to a serving dish, dressing and all, and serve with coleslaw, chipotle aioli, and warm tortillas on the side.

Note: At Ninfa's, all the seeds from dried peppers are repurposed. Here, they are used in a dressing, but they can be added to seasonings as well.

Curtido

- ¼ cup white vinegar
- 2 Tbsp olive oil
- 1 tsp granulated sugar
- 1 tsp salt
- ¼ tsp dried oregano
- ¼ tsp dried basil
- ¼ tsp ground cumin
- ¼ tsp black pepper
- ¼ tsp garlic powder
- ½ carrot, thinly sliced
- 1 stalk celery, cut into ¼-inch-thick slices
- ½ jicama, peeled and cut into ½-inch cubes
- 1 thick slice pineapple, cubed
- 1 chile de árbol

Tomatillo salsa

- 2 tomatillos
- 1 jalapeño pepper, stemmed
- ½ white onion, quartered
- 1 clove garlic
- Salt and black pepper

Queso asado

- 2 (1-inch-thick) square slices panela
- Olive oil, for drizzling
- 1 cup Tomatillo Salsa (see here)
- 1 cup Curtido (see here)
- 1 avocado, sliced
- 2 charred jalapeño peppers, seeded and cut into strips
- ½ cup pickled red onion (store-bought), for serving
- 4 tortillas, warmed, for serving

Queso Asado

SERVES 4 The charred queso at The Original Ninfa's on Navigation—served in a warm tortilla with blistered jalapeño, refreshing jicama, and salsas—is a chorus line of flavors. The panela, a curd-style frying cheese, is seared in a pan until it's gooey and oozy (while still retaining its shape). Padilla's version of *curtido*, a quick-pickled relish popular in Central America, is fruity with pineapple.

Curtido In a large saucepan, combine vinegar, oil, sugar, salt, dried herbs, and spices. Pour in 1 cup water and bring to a boil.

Add garlic, carrot, celery, jicama, pineapple, and chile, then remove from heat and let sit for 1 hour to cool and infuse the flavors into the vegetables. Curtido keeps, submerged in its liquid, in the fridge for up to 1 week.

Tomatillo salsa Preheat oven to 450°F.

On a baking sheet, stir together tomatillos, jalapeño, onion, and garlic, then roast for 10 minutes or until softened and charred.

Transfer to a blender and gently pulse until salsa-like. (Alternatively, transfer to a molcajete and smash together with a tejolote.) Season with salt and pepper.

Queso asado Cut each panela square in half diagonally to make 4 triangles. Drizzle oil over cheese.

In a frying pan set over high heat, pan-fry cheese for 1 minute. Flip and cook for another minute. (At the restaurant, the cheese is cooked in the wood-fired oven.) Transfer cheese hot to a serving tray and surround with tomatillo salsa, curtido, avocado, jalapeños, pickled red onion, and tortillas.

Peli Peli

PAUL FRIEDMAN

⭐ When chef Paul Friedman moved to Houston from his hometown of Johannesburg back in the eighties, he couldn't have chosen a better city. "Houston is very much like South Africa," Friedman says. "They both have so many cultural influences from all around the world." But Peli Peli happens to be the first South African restaurant in town.

The restaurant opened in 2009 in Vintage Park. A colorful rendition of an acacia tree in the dining room creates imposing ambiance in the lofty space, while decorative panels along the wall featuring the twelve tribes of Israel make for remarkable decor.

Friedman's cuisine is a fascinating mix of exotic fruits (mango, passion fruit, and guava), South African ingredients such as Peppadew and peri peri peppers, and abundant spices. The menu offers everything from house-cured *biltong* (South Africa's answer to beef jerky) to pan-seared seabass and char-grilled marinated rib eye. *Espetadas*—skewers of beef, chicken, or seafood, dangling dramatically from a metal frame and dripping with sauces like the Huguenot, a moreish melt of blue cheese, bacon, and raspberry—are most popular.

A second and third Peli Peli restaurant opened in The Galleria and Katy respectively. As a fast-casual spinoff, Peli Peli Kitchen was launched in 2016 with a menu that embraces the same distinctive cuisine, expressed in quick-lunch favorites such as peri peri flame-grilled chicken and marinated fajita-style beef, either served on its own or wrapped in naan.

No matter which Peli Peli you pick, you're always treated to food that is never too spicy, never too sweet, and always bursting with flavor.

1 lb chicken livers, cut into 1-inch pieces

Juice of 1 lemon

1 Tbsp vegetable oil

½ onion, finely chopped

½ red bell pepper, seeded, deveined, and finely chopped

½ yellow bell pepper, seeded, deveined, and finely chopped

½ green bell pepper, seeded, deveined, and finely chopped

1 clove garlic, finely chopped

2 Roma tomatoes, finely chopped

½ tsp chili powder

2 tsp Peli Peli seasoning (or Malay or Caribbean curry powder)

½ tsp ground paprika

1 cup chicken stock

1 Tbsp chopped cilantro, plus extra for garnish

Lemon wedges, for garnish (optional)

Steamed basmati rice, to serve (optional)

Toasted ciabatta, sliced (optional)

Curried Chicken Livers

SERVES 4 AS A MAIN (OR 6 TO 8 AS AN APPETIZER) Chicken livers are listed on the Peli Peli menu as a side dish; however, these zippy, velvety-soft bites hold their own as a main when served with rice. Friedman uses his own seasoning (available at the restaurant), but feel free to play around with an Indian masala, a Malay or Caribbean curry, or even your favorite seasoning.

In a bowl, toss chicken livers with lemon juice to coat well. Let sit for 20 minutes.

Heat oil in a large frying pan over medium-high heat. Add onion and bell peppers and sauté for 5 minutes. Add garlic and tomatoes and cook for another 5 minutes, stirring occasionally.

Drain chicken livers, then add them to the pan. Stir in chili powder, Peli Peli seasoning (or curry powder), and paprika. Mix well and cook for another 2 minutes. Pour in the stock. Reduce heat to medium-low and cook for 6 to 8 minutes, stirring occasionally. Turn off heat and set aside to cool in the pan for 5 minutes. Stir in cilantro and transfer to a serving platter. Garnish with cilantro and lemon wedges and with rice for a main. Alternatively, serve with toasted ciabatta as an appetizer.

Curried meat

1 Tbsp vegetable oil

1 yellow onion, chopped

½ red bell pepper, seeded, deveined, and chopped

½ yellow bell pepper, seeded, deveined, and chopped

½ green bell pepper, seeded, deveined, and chopped

2 cloves garlic, finely chopped

Sprig of rosemary

1 bay leaf

1 tsp paprika

1 tsp ground turmeric

1 tsp black pepper

½ tsp ground coriander

½ tsp ground cinnamon

½ Tbsp grated ginger

1 Tbsp Peli Peli seasoning (or Malay or Caribbean curry powder)

1 lb ground beef

1 cup tomato passata

½ cup apple juice

1 Tbsp mango chutney

1 tsp granulated sugar

Juice of ½ lemon

½ cup raisins

Salt

Custard topping

2 large eggs

½ cup whole milk

Salt and black pepper

Bobotie

SERVES 3 TO 4 If you love shepherd's pie, you're likely to go crazy for this curried meat dish. *Bobotie* (pronounced as "bah-boor-tea") is a comforting South African staple that can be paired with steamed rice or mash potatoes for a satisfying meal. Chef Paul Friedman serves it in a ramekin, topped with a layer of carrot *bredie* (at Peli Peli, that's a mash of carrots, leeks, and potatoes) and covered with a flaky pastry crust (see photo). For home cooks, the chef offers a classic custard topping as an effortless alternative.

Curried meat Heat oil in a large frying pan over medium heat. Add onion and bell peppers and sauté for 3 minutes. Add garlic and cook for another 2 minutes. Add rosemary, bay leaf, paprika, turmeric, black pepper, coriander, cinnamon, ginger, and Peli Peli seasoning (or curry powder). Stir for 2 minutes. Add beef, increase heat to high, and cook for 5 minutes.

Reduce heat to medium. Stir in passata, apple juice, chutney, sugar, lemon juice, and raisins. Cover and reduce heat to low. Cook for 30 minutes, stirring regularly to prevent the mixture from sticking to the bottom. Remove the pan from the heat and let sit for 15 minutes. Skim off the fat gathered on the surface. Season with salt.

Custard topping Lightly whisk eggs in a bowl for 1 minute. Add milk and whisk for another minute. Season with salt and pepper.

Assembly Preheat oven to 400°F.

Fill a 9- × 13-inch casserole dish three-quarters full with curried meat and even out into a single layer. Tilt the casserole dish slightly and move it around gently, to evenly spread the custard topping on top. Bake for 30 minutes or until the top is colored and forms a crust. Serve.

Poitín Bar + Kitchen

DOMINICK LEE

⭐ If you've got it, flaunt it! With its lofty dining spaces and an inviting patio boasting sweeping views of Houston's downtown skyline, this sleek cocktail bar stands out in Houston's art district. Add to that a long list of craft cocktails, inspired food, and stunning desserts, and its popularity is easy to understand.

Poitín is named after an Irish moonshine whiskey, a nod to owner Ian Tucker's home country, Ireland. And yes, it is on the drink menu: the Lion's Kiss is a kicking-good concoction made with blood orange and Drumlish Poitín.

The food menu narrates chef Dominick Lee's commitment to whole-animal cooking and locally sourced ingredients, as well as his fascination with global cuisines. Lee brings a range of bold flavors to it, from inventive interpretations of Creole staples (for instance, "dirty" mushrooms mingled with chicken livers) to an ever-adventurous play with vegetables, as in chipotle-pickled cauliflower, and the collards liquor (the green's braising liquids) used to flavor risotto.

The Louisiana native loves his seafood, also evidenced by the menu, which includes charbroiled oysters, grilled fish collar, and a seafood charcuterie with a changing selection of smoky fish rillettes, pickled shrimp, and fish pastrami. Don't overlook the whole market fish: it's a stunning presentation of the crispiest, freshest Gulf fish.

On a sweeter note, pastry chef Hani Lae delivers on globally inspired desserts such as a shatteringly crisp peach and walnut baklava, and a coffee and chocolate baba with passion fruit and banana.

Poitín embraces Houston's vibrant immigrant culture in mouthwatering manner. Tucker explains, "That multicultural spirit from our team enables us to create our unique global offering."

¼ cup (½ stick) butter

3 shallots, finely chopped

5 Tbsp lemon juice

¼ cup white wine

Pinch of saffron

25 to 30 PEI mussels,
   scrubbed clean,
   debearded, and
   rinsed well

6 cherry tomatoes, halved

Salt and black pepper

Fennel fronds, for garnish

Toasted sourdough,
   to serve

Mussels in Shallot-Saffron Broth

SERVES 2 Mussels, inexpensive and quick to cook, are made for sharing. Dominick Lee's version marries tender mussels with a delicate, saffron-perfumed broth, delicious served with toasted bread.

Melt butter in a saucepan over medium heat. Add shallots and sauté for 2 minutes. Add lemon juice and wine and cook for another 2 minutes. Add saffron and cook for 1 minute to release its aroma.

Discard any mussels that are broken or do not shut when tapped. Add mussels and tomatoes to the shallot-saffron broth and cook for 5 minutes, or until the mussels have opened. Discard any mussels that have not opened.

Season with salt and pepper. Spoon mussels and tomatoes into a serving bowl and ladle in the broth. Garnish with fennel fronds. Serve hot with toasted sourdough.

Simple syrup

1 cup granulated sugar

Fiddle fern

1½ oz unaged apple brandy (preferably Copper & Kings)

¾ oz vermouth (preferably Dolin Blanc)

½ oz sherry (preferably Tio Pepe Fino)

2 tsp Simple Syrup (see here)

2 dashes grapefruit bitters (preferably Bittermens Hopped)

2 drops orange blossom water (preferably Cortas), for finishing

Granny Smith apple, very thinly sliced, for garnish

Dehydrated apple wheel, for garnish

Fiddle Fern Cocktail

SERVES 1 Houston mixologist Sarah Cuneo is an expert at crafting cocktails that impress. Not only is she a seasoned cocktail maker, Cuneo is an accomplished violinist and poet. It might explain why her inventively named cocktails like Creature's Folly and Siren's Purl seem so lyrical. The refreshing Fiddle Fern is a velvety smooth apple brandy cocktail, with a subtle hint of grapefruit.

Simple syrup In a saucepan, combine sugar and 1 cup water and heat through until sugar is dissolved. Set aside to cool to room temperature. Refrigerate until needed.

Fiddle fern Use a jigger cup (cocktail measure) to measure ingredients. Place brandy, vermouth, sherry, simple syrup, and grapefruit bitters in a pint glass and add ice cubes. Using a cocktail spoon, stir for 1 minute. (This will chill the liquid and releases the aromas.)

Strain cocktail into a frozen cocktail glass filled with ice. Add orange blossom water, arrange apple slices against the rim, and float dehydrated apple wheel on top.

Pondicheri

ANITA JAISINGHANI

★ The original Pondicheri in Upper Kirby is a vibrant and lofty industrial-style space, a contemporary Indian restaurant offering craveable fare. Chef-owner Anita Jaisinghani is beloved for her modern take on *chaat*, Indian street food, a signature that earned her James Beard Award nominations for best chef and best new restaurant. Rooted in ancient Indian recipes and techniques, her food is healthful as well as invigoratingly delicious. "Food is the new medicine," Jaisinghani says. "I like to make tasty food that nourishes the body and makes us feels good. This is my new frontier."

Inspired by India's many regional cuisines, Jaisinghani's kaleidoscopic menu of warmly spiced dishes include all-day breakfast favorites like dosa stuffed with sautéed greens and avocado masala, as well as her popular thali, each a bountiful spread of fragrant curries and condiments arranged in individual cups on a tray.

Upstairs from the restaurant, the Bake Lab + Shop is bright and uplifting with its sunshine orange accents. It offers baked goods such as spongy doughnuts soused with homemade rose-cardamom-saffron syrup, and crisp turmeric-and-cumin-spiced shortbread. Breakfast and lunch items are also served, like moringa (the "new" power green) maple pancakes and a wild-yeast sourdough grilled cheese with mushroom masala.

In 2016, Jaisinghani opened a second Pondicheri in New York City, which is managed by her daughter, Ajna Jai. And in 2018, she opened her third location, Pondi Café, in Houston's Asia Society Texas Center, with more Pondi offshoots in the making.

ove,
, black
ddy w/
+ sugar
eet
-mace syrup

o drinks

BOOZE

our beer is
all TX, all the time
12 oz. ca $5.
our wines are seasonal;
see offerings
on paper
menu

·mim
g
p

·seas
g
p

PONDICHER

Nonstick cooking spray, for greasing

¾ cup (1½ sticks) butter

1½ cups granulated sugar

1½ cups khoya or ricotta (see headnote), finely crumbled

4 large eggs

1 tsp kewra water (see Note)

¾ cup heavy cream (divided)

2 cups all-purpose flour

⅓ cup semolina

½ Tbsp ground cardamom

½ Tbsp baking powder

¼ tsp salt

½ cup roasted pistachios, chopped, for garnish (optional)

Note: Kewra is an extract distilled from the pandanus (or screw pine) plant. It adds a floral fragrance. You can find bottled kewra water at Fiesta, Phoenicia Specialty Foods, and Indian supermarkets.

Mawa Cakes

MAKES 12   This Indian cheesecake is made with *khoya*, a dry, soft cheese made from dried milk, which can be found in Indian supermarkets in Hillcroft. Ricotta is a good substitute, but it'll need a little help: heat the ricotta in a pan over low heat for 2 minutes or until it is thick, dry, and crumbly.

Preheat oven to 350°F. Grease two 6-cup muffin pans with cooking spray.

In a stand mixer fitted with the paddle attachment, combine butter and sugar and mix on high speed for 2 minutes or until creamy. Add khoya (or ricotta) and mix for another minute. Add eggs one at a time, mixing on medium speed after each addition. Increase speed to high and mix for 1 to 2 minutes.

Add kewra water and ½ cup cream and mix until just fully incorporated.

In a bowl, combine flour, semolina, cardamom, baking powder, and salt. Add a little to the stand mixer and mix well. Gradually add the remaining mixture until batter is smooth and homogenous.

Using a ½-cup measuring cup, scoop batter into the muffin molds. Bake for 25 minutes or until a toothpick inserted into the center comes out clean.

Remove the pan from the oven and, using a toothpick, poke a few holes in each cake and drizzle the remaining ¼ cup heavy cream overtop. Sprinkle with pistachios, if using, then let cakes sit for a few minutes to cool. Serve.

Cilantro chutney

- 2 large bunches cilantro, rinsed under cold running water
- 1 serrano pepper, stemmed, plus extra to taste
- ½ Granny Smith apple, unpeeled, cored, and sliced
- ½ cup unsalted dry-roasted peanuts
- 1 cup plain full-fat yogurt
- Juice of 1 lemon
- 1 tsp salt, plus extra to taste

Carrot roti

- 2 cups atta flour, plus extra for dusting (see headnote)
- 1 small red onion, finely chopped
- 1 carrot, grated
- ½ bunch cilantro, chopped
- 1 Tbsp clarified butter (ghee), plus extra for spreading
- 1 tsp ajwain (carom) seeds (see Note)
- 1 tsp salt
- 1 tsp black pepper
- 2 Tbsp vegetable oil
- Plain yogurt, to serve
- Cilantro Chutney (see here)
- 8 fried eggs, to serve (optional)
- Sprigs of cilantro, for garnish

Carrot Roti with Cilantro Chutney

SERVES 8 "Roti is quintessential unleavened Indian flatbreads, and every region has its own version," says chef Anita Jaisinghani. At home, she adds finely grated carrot or beet to the dough, then serves it with a fried egg, cilantro chutney, and a dollop of yogurt for the perfect breakfast. Atta flour, which is available at Indian supermarkets, is the best flour to use. It can be substituted with whole-wheat pastry flour or any other fine-ground wheat flour. (Regular whole-wheat flour is too coarsely ground.)

Cilantro chutney Discard bottom 4 inches of cilantro stems. Shake cilantro to remove excess water and set aside.

In a blender, blend serrano pepper, apple, peanuts, yogurt, lemon juice, and salt on low speed, slowly increasing speed to high, until mixture is completely smooth. Add cilantro, half a bunch at a time, and blend until smooth. Season with more salt and serrano. (Makes 2 cups.) Store chutney in an airtight container in the refrigerator for up to 2 days.

Carrot roti In a mixing bowl, combine flour, onion, carrot, cilantro, ghee, ajwain seeds, salt, and pepper. Add 1 cup water and knead until mixture turns to a soft dough. Add more water (1 tablespoon at a time) as you go, kneading until the dough naturally forms a supple ball. Knead oil into the dough until smooth and pliable. Shape into a ball, then let sit for 30 minutes to relax the gluten. Divide into 8 equal portions and shape each into a small ball.

Assembly Preheat a frying pan over medium-high heat. Roll a portion of dough into a 6-inch circle. Place in the pan and cook for 2 minutes or until bubbles form on the cooked side. Flip roti and cook for another 2 minutes or until bubbles form. Spread ghee on the top side and transfer to a dish towel–lined plate. Wrap to keep roti warm and repeat with the remaining roti dough. Serve immediately with yogurt, cilantro chutney, and a fried egg. Garnish with cilantro.

> **Note:** Ajwain (or carom) is an aromatic spice popular for its digestive benefits (just one of its many benefits, in fact). The seeds are used whole (raw or roasted), ground into a paste, or soaked to make ajwain water.

Ristorante Cavour

MAURIZIO FERRARESE

★ Walking into Hotel Granduca is like setting foot in an Italian palazzo without ever leaving Houston. From the hand-painted walls and ceilings to the secluded garden with its sculptures and sparkling pool, the hotel oozes opulence in a warm and welcoming way.

Chef Maurizio Ferrarese hails from Piemonte, the same northern Italian region as the hotel's owner, Giorgio Borlenghi. Ferrarese attended culinary school just north of the Langhe wine region, famous for its Barolo and Barbaresco wines, both of which line up in the hotel's award-winning wine cellar.

Nestled inside the 130-room luxury boutique hotel is Ristorante Cavour, accented with Murano-glass chandeliers and original paintings, heirlooms from Borlenghi's family. Cavour's sophisticated menu, under the watchful eye of the talented chef, is renowned for the Piemontese culinary experience it offers—and that comes with enjoying the freshest ingredients sourced from as close by as possible. For Ferrarese, that means lettuces from peri-urban farm Verdegreens in Houston, shrimp from Galveston Bay, and wagyu beef from Strube Ranch in Pittsburg, Texas. This is where you can twirl your fork in thin ribbons of buttery-soft, yolk-rich *tajarin*, or polish off creamy risotto rich with porcini and the Langhe's favorite soft-ripened robiola cheese. But first, peruse the antipasti. The Piemonte region is, after all, credited for inventing the antipasti, among which is the iconic *vitello tonnato*, at Cavour a delectable version of sous-vide veal and fresh yellow fin tuna, cloaked with the creamiest of tuna-caper sauces.

Ferrarese loves living and cooking in Houston: "I can put rabbit on the menu and people will order it," he says.

▶ **Langoustine Risotto with Meyer Lemon and Capers** | p. 174–75

Powdered capers

1 Tbsp capers

2 Tbsp extra-virgin olive oil

Risotto

8 fresh langoustines

3 Tbsp extra-virgin olive oil (divided)

2 cups carnaroli rice (preferably Acquerello)

Sea salt

½ cup (1 stick) butter, cut into ½-inch cubes

½ cup grated Parmesan

Grated zest and juice of 1 Meyer lemon

Langoustine Risotto with Meyer Lemon and Capers

SERVES 4 Born and raised in Vercelli (the home of carnaroli rice), chef Maurizio Ferrarese knows how to make risotto. Follow his lead and (re)discover risotto as a wowing dish that you can have on the table in 30 minutes, including prep. The absence of stock may throw off some risotto makers, but believe me, this version is full of flavor, brightened as it is with Meyer lemon and briny fried capers, and finished with sweet, succulent langoustine. Speaking of which, if you can't find langoustines (try Central Market), use lobster tails or Gulf shrimp.

Powdered capers Pat dry the capers with paper towel. Heat oil in a small frying pan over high heat. Drop a caper into the pan; if it sizzles right away, the oil is hot enough. Add capers to the pan and fry for 1 minute or until crispy. Drain on a paper towel–lined plate. Let sit for 2 minutes to cool, then crumble capers between your fingers to a coarse powder. Set aside.

Risotto Remove shells from the langoustines and chop the meat into ½-inch pieces. Set aside.

Bring 6 cups water to a boil in a medium saucepan. Reduce heat to medium-low and hold it at a low simmer.

Heat 2 tablespoons oil in a saucepan over medium heat. Add rice and warm until the rice feels hot to the touch but hasn't browned. Increase heat to medium-high and add 3 ladles of boiling water and a pinch of salt. Using a wooden spoon, stir rice until all the water is incorporated, making sure no grains stick to the side of the pan. Add another 3 to 4 ladles of hot water, another pinch of salt, and stir. Repeat this process for at least 13 minutes or until al dente and the grains have swollen in a thick, glossy liquid. If the rice is still chalky, add a little more hot water and cook for another 2 minutes. Remove from heat.

Stir in butter, Parmesan, and chopped langoustines. (They will cook in the residual heat.) Season with lemon zest and juice. Stir in the remaining 1 tablespoon oil, remove from heat, and let sit for 5 minutes.

Assembly

1 Tbsp olive oil

8 langoustines, peeled

Risotto (see here)

Salt and black pepper

Powdered Capers
  (see here)

1 Tbsp finely chopped
  chives

Microgreens, for garnish

Grated lemon zest,
  for garnish

Assembly Heat oil in a frying pan for 1 minute over high heat. Add langoustines and toss for 2 minutes or until lightly seared on all sides and cooked through. Set aside.

Stir 1 tablespoon hot water into the risotto to create a loose, fluid texture known as *all'onda*, which means wavy or "creating waves." Season with salt and pepper.

Divide among four plates, garnish with a sprinkle of each of powdered capers and chives, and arrange the lightly seared langoustines on top. Garnish with microgreens and lemon zest. Serve immediately.

Braised beef

1 (2-lb) grass-fed beef chuck (preferably wagyu), trimmed of excess fat

Salt and black pepper

6 Tbsp extra-virgin olive oil

1 large onion, finely chopped

1 large carrot, finely chopped

2 stalks celery, finely chopped

1 cup Barolo wine

4 ripe tomatoes, peeled and puréed

2 sprigs thyme

4 leaves sage

Carrots

20 baby heirloom carrots, peeled (see Note)

3 Tbsp extra-virgin olive oil

1 to 2 tsp sea salt

Barolo-Braised Beef with Heirloom Carrots and Charred Cipollini Onion

SERVES 4 Fork-tender wagyu beef, slow-cooked in a Barolo wine, pairs perfectly—you guessed it—with the same wine! At home, grass-fed beef (preferably from a local rancher) braised in a red of your choice will deliver beautifully on those rich, comforting flavors too. And the great thing about this dish? You can put it in the oven and forget about it for a few hours.

Braised beef Preheat oven to 300°F.

Generously season beef with salt and pepper.

Heat oil in a large Dutch oven over medium-high heat. Add beef and sear for 2 minutes on each side or until browned all over. Transfer beef to a plate.

In the same pot set over medium heat, cook onion, carrot, and celery for 3 to 5 minutes, until lightly caramelized. Increase heat to high, pour in wine, and cook for 5 minutes or until the liquid has evaporated. Add puréed tomatoes, the beef, and enough boiling water to just cover the beef. Season with salt and pepper, add the thyme and sage, and cover. Cook in the oven for 3 to 4 hours, until meat is tender enough to be easily pierced with a fork. Remove beef from the sauce and put it into a bowl.

Bring the sauce to a boil over high heat, reduce heat to medium, and cook for 2 to 3 minutes, until the sauce is thick enough to coat the back of a spoon. Return beef to the sauce and keep warm until ready to serve.

Carrots Preheat oven to 450°F.

In a bowl, toss carrots with oil and salt to coat, then spread out in a single layer on a baking sheet. Roast for 5 minutes. Remove from the oven, toss, and return to the oven to roast for another 5 minutes or until carrots are softened and lightly charred.

Note: If you cannot find baby heirloom carrots, simply use rainbow carrots, quartered lengthwise.

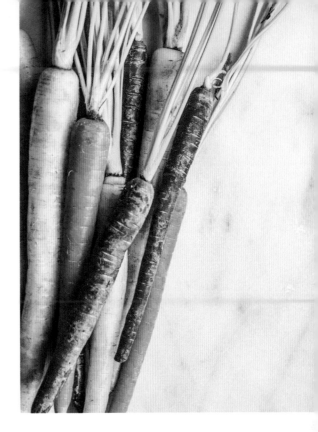

Cipollini onions

12 cipollini onions

2 Tbsp extra-virgin
olive oil

1 tsp sea salt

Fingerling purée

2 lbs fingerling potatoes,
peeled

Salt

½ cup (1 stick) butter,
cut into cubes

½ cup warm milk, plus
extra as needed

2 Tbsp extra-virgin
olive oil

Cipollini onions Preheat oven to 450°F.

Bring a small saucepan of water to a boil, add onions, and boil for 30 seconds. Drain, then set aside to cool. Peel onions.

In a bowl, gently toss onions with oil and salt to coat. Arrange onions, with the tops facing up, in a single layer on a baking sheet and roast for 15 to 20 minutes, until softened and charred (no need to turn).

Fingerling purée Put the potatoes into a saucepan, cover with cold water, and add a pinch of salt. Bring to a boil and cook for 10 minutes or until cooked through. Drain, then pass potatoes through a ricer (or use a masher for a coarser consistency). Add butter, a little at a time, then warm milk. Season with salt. Add more milk if you prefer a creamier consistency. Stir in oil.

Assembly Using a slotted spoon, transfer the hot beef to a cutting board and cut into 1-inch slices. Spoon fingerling purée onto the center of four plates, place sliced beef on top, and arrange carrots and onions around it. Spoon sauce overtop and serve. (Alternatively, serve the braised beef, roasted carrots, and onions family-style on a beautiful platter, with the purée and sauce on the side.)

Rudyard's Pub

JORDAN ECONOMY

★ As Houston's bar scene evolves with plushy new establishments, one watering hole remains a trusted constant—a place where a good burger and a beer come with a side of history and a heap of character. For more than forty years, Rudyard's Pub ("Rudz" for short) has been a home for lovers of craft beers. "We've been in the microbrew game in Texas since craft beers were produced in Texas," says Lelia Rodgers (owner since 1993). "And we've helped them grow!" Today the pub boasts thirty-six beers on tap, with roughly three-quarters of them devoted to local beers. Rodgers also hosted monthly beer dinners long before that was even a thing in Houston. And from the moment she opened up the pub's second floor, in 1996, Rudz became a hub for local bands, spoken-word events, and poetry nights. (Fun fact: Rodgers is the president of Public Poetry.)

In 2018, chef Jordan Economy, a Rudz regular since 2005, took the kitchen reins. Economy ramped up the existing menu with notable offerings such as hearty boudin balls stuffed with cheese, and nachos heaped with crispy-fried oysters, salsa verde, hot sauce, and pickled red cabbage. With this menu, Economy shows a love for bold flavors and a little Louisiana heat. (But you wouldn't expect less from a New Orleanian, right?)

Rudyard's bimonthly Chef's Table series (the next chapter in an ongoing series of original beer dinners) features a tasting menu paired with local brews. This is when Economy really shines with inspiration and when you'll see anything from house-made chorizo ravioli to beetroot-marinated octopus. At Rudyard's, beer food is seriously kicked up a notch.

Scallion mustard

Bunch of scallions, cut into 1½-inch pieces

⅓ cup white balsamic or apple cider vinegar

½ Tbsp honey

½ cup Creole mustard

¼ cup extra-virgin olive oil

¼ cup canola oil

Seasoned panko

2 cups panko breadcrumbs

1 Tbsp finely grated Parmesan

½ Tbsp garlic powder

1 tsp ground turmeric

¼ tsp salt

¼ tsp black pepper

Scotch eggs

10 large eggs, room temperature (divided)

1 lb 70/30 Angus ground beef (see Note on page 180)

1 Tbsp salt

1 tsp black pepper

1 tsp ground turmeric

1 tsp onion powder

1 tsp garlic powder

1 tsp chili flakes

1 tsp Cajun seasoning

1½ cups all-purpose flour, for dredging

2 cups Seasoned Panko (see here)

Canola or peanut oil, for deep-frying

1 cup Scallion Mustard (see here)

Scotch Egg with Scallion Mustard

MAKES 8 You know you have a skillfully made Scotch egg when the soft yolk oozes out as soon as you cut the egg open. Perhaps you already have your own foolproof method for soft-boiled eggs. If not, follow this recipe's lead. The rest is child's play: wrap the yolky gems in blankets of seasoned ground beef, bread them, and into the fryer they go.

Scallion mustard In a blender, blend scallions, vinegar, honey, and mustard until smooth. With the motor still running, slowly pour in both oils in a steady stream until emulsified. Transfer mixture to a bowl, cover, and refrigerate until needed.

Seasoned panko In a mixing bowl, combine all ingredients. Set aside.

Scotch eggs Add 8 eggs to a saucepan and add enough water to just cover them. Bring to a boil over medium-high heat and boil for exactly 6½ minutes (add 1 minute if you are using extra-large farmers' market eggs). Immediately drain and transfer eggs to a bowl of ice water to cool. Peel and set aside.

In a bowl, combine beef, salt, pepper, turmeric, onion and garlic powders, chili flakes, and Cajun seasoning. Divide beef mixture into 8 portions.

Put a portion of the beef mixture into the palm of your hand and pat it flat, making sure it's large enough to wrap around the egg. Place a peeled egg in the center and, using your hand, carefully mold the beef around it to cover completely. Repeat with the remaining cooked eggs and the portions of beef.

Put flour into a bowl. Crack the remaining 2 uncooked eggs into a second bowl and lightly beat. Add seasoned panko to a third bowl. Dredge the beef-encased eggs in the flour, then in the egg, and finally in the seasoned panko to coat all over.

Heat oil in a deep fryer to a temperature of 350°F. Working in batches to avoid overcrowding, carefully lower Scotch eggs into the oil and cook for 5 minutes or until they are crisp, golden, and rise to the surface.

To serve, cut the Scotch eggs in half and serve with scallion mustard on the side or on top.

Comeback sauce

2 cups mayonnaise (preferably Duke's)

¼ cup Louisiana hot sauce

¼ cup red wine vinegar

2 Tbsp chili sauce

1 Tbsp dried parsley

1 Tbsp dried oregano

1 Tbsp sweet relish

1 Tbsp Cajun seasoning

½ Tbsp chili powder

½ tsp prepared horseradish

Juice of 2 lemons

Candied bacon

2 cups packed dark brown sugar

¼ cup cayenne pepper

8 slices thick-cut bacon, room temperature

Waugh burger

1 lb 70/30 Angus ground beef (see Note)

Salt and black pepper

Candied Bacon (see here)

4 thin slices aged cheddar (preferably 5-year)

4 brioche buns

Butter, room temperature

Lettuce, tomato, sliced red onions, and pickled jalapeños, for garnish

The Waugh Burger

SERVES 4 A super-juicy, perfectly grilled beef patty crowned with candied bacon, perched on a brioche bun and hugged with comeback sauce, Rudyard's Waugh Burger is a burger you'll come back for. Jordan Economy's sauce is a tangy and spicy cross between Creole remoulade and Thousand Island dressing. And you'll love that it's an ample batch, because you'll want it on French fries, shrimp, crab cakes, and crispy Scotch eggs (page 179).

Comeback sauce In a bowl, combine all ingredients. Pour into a clean jar, cover, and refrigerate until needed or for up to 2 months. (Makes 2½ cups.)

Candied bacon Preheat oven to 350°F.

In a bowl, combine sugar and cayenne pepper. Coat bacon with sugar mixture and arrange in a single layer on a baking sheet. Bake for 12 to 14 minutes, until bacon is caramelized. Let rest until bacon hardens.

Assembly Preheat a barbecue grill over high heat. In a bowl, season beef with salt and pepper. Shape beef into 4 patties, about ½ inch thick, and grill for 3 minutes. Flip and grill for another 4 minutes for medium-rare (or 5 minutes for medium). Place a slice of cheddar on each patty to melt. Transfer patties to a plate and keep warm.

Slice brioche buns open and butter the cut sides. Place on the grill, butter side down, and toast for 30 seconds or until golden.

Slather comeback sauce on toasted sides of buns. Place a burger patty on the bottom half of each bun, top with lettuce, tomato, red onion, jalapeños, and candied bacon. Serve immediately.

> **Note:** At Rudyard's, the ground beef mix is a blend of chuck and beef cheek, which yields 70% lean meat patties. As long as the patties are at least 20% fat (and 80% lean), the patties will be succulent.

Saigon House

TONY J. NGUYEN

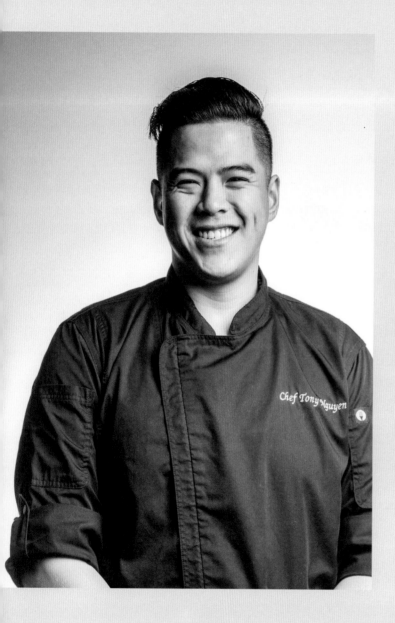

★ On the corner of Main and Rosalie in Midtown, Saigon House is abuzz not even a year after floods damaged the restaurant in August 2017. Tony J. Nguyen, who joined as culinary director immediately after Hurricane Harvey, revamped the restaurant and the menu.

Nguyen breathes contemporary life into his heritage cuisine, often finding ways to add Houston roots to classic Vietnamese dishes. These include a hearty oxtail and smoked brisket pho, and the mini *bánh xèo* tacos (crispy Vietnamese egg pancakes stuffed with marinated pork belly, shrimp, lettuce, and herbs) that won him first place at the 2018 Gr8 Taco Challenge.

Nguyen grew up in a Vietnamese community in southeast Houston, and even at a young age he indulged in the seasonal pleasure of eating crawfish. "My dad would buy a bag of crawfish from a local seafood shop, and I remember my mom peeling them for me as soon as the crawfish were dumped onto the newspaper-lined floor." It comes as no surprise that Viet-Cajun crawfish is one of his greatest hits. Saigon House serves crawfish in a variety of Viet-Cajun sauces, including fan favorites such as H-Town Bang and the racy Saigon Heat.

Nguyen continues to expand his menu, preparing the freshest of seafood with tantalizing Viet flavor combinations—spicy, sweet, salty, and sour—and always served with plentiful fresh herbs plucked from the restaurant's organic garden. It's just outside the kitchen door, and one of the things that underlines the intent of Saigon House: delivering fresh flavors, good ingredients, and lots of happy bows to childhood memories.

▶ **Viet Carpaccio with Herb Salad (Bò Tái Chanh)** | p. 184

Tenderloin	Fish-sauce vinaigrette	Herb salad	Assembly
1 lb beef tenderloin	¼ cup fish sauce	¼ cup chopped rice paddy herb (*ngò om*)	1 lime, quartered
Salt and black pepper	¼ cup granulated sugar	¼ cup chopped sawtooth coriander (*ngò gai*)	½ small red onion, thinly sliced
1 Tbsp butter	¼ cup lime juice	¼ cup roughly chopped arugula	1 Tbsp store-bought fried shallots
1 Tbsp vegetable oil	2 cloves garlic, finely chopped	2 to 3 Tbsp Fish-Sauce Vinaigrette (see here)	1 Tbsp finely chopped roasted peanuts
	1 bird's eye chile (optional), finely chopped		1 Tbsp diced tomatoes

Viet Carpaccio with Herb Salad (Bò Tái Chanh)

SERVES 4 The secret to this delightfully easy recipe is quality beef tenderloin, fresh aromatic herbs, and a hit of the vinaigrette that is equal parts pungent, sweet, tart, and spicy (it's a recipe from his aunt). Vietnamese supermarkets in Asiatown stock a wide variety of aromatic herbs (including *ngò om* and *ngò gai*) for us to discover and use in this salad, but this carpaccio is just as happy with cilantro, mint, and Thai basil, though, of course, the aromatic flavor will be slightly different.

Tenderloin Remove silver skin from the tenderloin. Season with salt and pepper.

Heat butter and oil in a large frying pan over high heat. Add tenderloin and sear for 30 seconds on each side or until lightly browned. Transfer tenderloin to a cutting board to cool for 2 to 3 minutes. Roll tenderloin in plastic wrap like a sausage. Freeze for 1 to 2 hours, until it feels firm (but not frozen) when you squeeze it gently.

Fish-sauce vinaigrette In a small saucepan, combine fish sauce and sugar and cook over medium heat until sugar is dissolved. Pour into a bowl and let cool for 30 minutes. Stir in lime juice, garlic, and chile, if using.

Herb salad In a bowl, toss herbs with vinaigrette.

Assembly Heat a frying pan over high heat. Pan-sear lime wedges for 30 seconds on each side.

Using a sharp knife, thinly slice chilled tenderloin. Arrange slices in a circle, slightly overlapping them. Place a mound of herb salad on top, then garnish with onion, fried shallots, peanuts, tomatoes, and seared lime wedges.

Marinade

½ cup granulated sugar

1 (12-fl oz) can Coco Rico soda

6 Tbsp fish sauce

2 Tbsp oyster sauce

1 ½ tsp onion powder

Caramelized pork

1 (2-lb) skinless pork belly

4 large eggs

¼ cup chopped scallions, for garnish

Steamed rice, to serve

Sautéed mustard greens, to serve

Note: The pork belly braising liquid is very fatty. If you'd like to use this as extra sauce, cool it in the refrigerator first and then skim off the layer of fat that has consolidated on the surface. In a saucepan, bring the sauce to a boil and reduce until syrupy.

Caramelized Pork (Thit Kho Tàu)

SERVES 4 This caramelized pork recipe is a personal favorite of chef Tony J. Nguyen's. "Growing up, my mom didn't have much time, so she would make a big pot of *thit kho tàu* to last a few meals," he says. "While other kids were eating cereal for breakfast, I had a bowl of *thit kho tàu*. I suspect almost every Vietnamese kid here has had the same experience." At Saigon House, it's a special order, sliced, charred crisp, and served as bao sliders.

Marinade Melt sugar in a medium saucepan, untouched, gently tilting the pan a little to distribute the sugar across the bottom. Cook over medium-high heat for 1 minute or until lightly caramelized. Pour in Coco Rico and stir to mix. Add fish sauce, oyster sauce, and onion powder and cook for 1 minute. Remove from heat and divide the mixture between two bowls.

Caramelized pork If you have an immersion circulator, set the temperature to 65.6°C (150.08°F). Pour the marinade from one of the bowls into a vacuum-sealed bag and add pork belly. Seal and sous-vide for 18 hours or until tender. (Alternatively, pour marinade from one of the bowls into a crockpot and add pork belly, fat side up. Cook on the high setting for 1 hour, then change to the low setting and cook for 5 hours.) Fill a large bowl with ice water. Place the pork belly in the ice bath, then transfer to a plate.

Bring a small saucepan of water to a boil. Add eggs and boil on medium-high heat for 5 minutes. Transfer eggs to a bowl of ice water and let sit for 20 seconds to cool. Peel eggs and keep in a bowl in cold water in the refrigerator until needed.

Heat a large frying pan over medium heat. Sear pork belly, fat-side down, for 5 minutes, moving it around occasionally to prevent it from burning. Sear for 2 minutes on each remaining side.

Drain fat from the pan, then add marinade from the second bowl. Increase heat to medium-high and cook pork belly for 1½ minutes. Flip and cook for another 1 ½ minutes. Add whole eggs and cook for 2 minutes or until sauce is reduced and syrupy.

Transfer pork belly to a cutting board and slice. Arrange pork in four serving bowls, spoon sauce overtop, and add an egg to each bowl. Garnish with scallions and serve with rice and mustard greens.

Saint Arnold Brewing Co.

RYAN SAVOIE

⭐ Saint Arnold is Houston's oldest microbrewery, but there is nothing micro about its new restaurant and beer garden's style. Grand arched alcoves and the high-vaulted ceiling with wood-beamed supports and wrought-iron chandeliers remind one of a medieval church. Six local artists were commissioned to paint abstract murals for the dining room. Outside, the colossal steel-framed beer garden fits in with its industrial surroundings, complete with an intimate view of the brewery's fermentation tanks and Houston's skyline beyond.

Executive chef Ryan Savoie has been with Saint Arnold since 2012. "I get to work with ingredients from right here in the brewery—that you don't get in an average restaurant," he shares. The pizza dough is made with beer, and the loose grains are added to the breading for chicken. He uses Saint Arnold Root Beer in a brine for pork chops, adds hops to caramel, and has a malted crème brûlée on the dessert menu. "I don't shoehorn beer into everything on the menu. Malt is sweet, and hops are bitter. Finding a place for them in food takes a little trial and error." The delectable menu comes with a dose of wit: fresh-baked pretzels and queso are described as "the stuff that dreams are made of... if dreams involve water, grain, and yeast," and the *"Ach du Lieber"* weekly wurst is prepared in the "friendly confines of [the] Saint Arnold kitchen." Being a brewery, there is a solid pairing with each menu item.

▶ **Chicken-Fried Pickled Green Tomatoes** | p. 188 **and Crawfish Rolls** | p. 189

Pickled tomatoes

1 carrot, roughly chopped

1 yellow onion, roughly chopped

2 cloves garlic, chopped

¼ cup kosher salt

1 Tbsp mustard seeds

1 Tbsp whole allspice

½ Tbsp black peppercorns

A few sprigs of dill

4 cups white vinegar

4 cups granulated sugar

5 green (unripe) tomatoes, cut into ½-inch-thick slices

Seasoned flour

1½ cups panko breadcrumbs

1 cup all-purpose flour (divided)

1 Tbsp kosher salt

1 Tbsp black pepper

1 tsp cayenne pepper

Chicken-fried pickled tomatoes

2 cups all-purpose flour (divided), plus extra for dusting and dredging

2 cups buttermilk (divided)

2 eggs (divided)

2½ cups Seasoned Flour (see here)

Pickled Tomatoes (see here)

2 qts peanut or canola oil, for deep-frying

Dipping sauce, to serve

Chicken-Fried Pickled Green Tomatoes

SERVES 10 TO 12 The "chicken fried" here refers to the seasoned flour used in the coating. "More often than not, green tomatoes are fried in cornmeal, as that's the Southern manner," explains chef Ryan Savoie. "Somebody's auntie or grandmother would most certainly start fanning herself and declare 'Land sakes!' or 'Good heavens!' upon seeing these. Don't worry, though. Life is too beautiful to be completely bound by tradition."

Pickled tomatoes Put all ingredients except tomatoes into a saucepan. Pour in 2 cups water and cook over medium-high heat for 5 minutes, stirring occasionally to make sure sugar and salt are dissolved.

Place tomatoes in a large container and pour in hot pickling mixture, leaving a little room at the top of the container. Cover container and let sit for at least 4 hours. (Leftover tomatoes can be stored in an airtight container in the refrigerator for up to 1 week.)

Seasoned flour In a large bowl, combine all ingredients.

Chicken-fried pickled tomatoes Dust a baking sheet with flour. Put 1 cup flour into a shallow bowl, whisk 1 cup buttermilk with 1 egg in a second bowl, and put 1¼ cups seasoned flour into a third bowl.

Dredge a tomato slice in the plain flour, then in buttermilk, and finally in the seasoned flour to coat. Place tomato on the prepared baking sheet and repeat with the remaining tomato slices. Replenish the bowls with fresh flour, buttermilk-egg mixture, and seasoned flour as needed. Let tomatoes sit for 30 minutes (otherwise the coating will slide right off when you bite into them.)

Meanwhile, heat oil in a deep fryer or deep saucepan to a temperature of 350°F. (Use a fryer thermometer to monitor the temperature.)

Working in small batches to avoid overcrowding, carefully lower tomatoes into the pan. Deep-fry for 4 to 5 minutes, until tomatoes are golden brown. Using a slotted spoon, transfer tomatoes to a paper towel–lined tray. Let cool slightly.

Serve with your favorite dipping sauce, like remoulade.

1½ cups mayonnaise

½ cup finely chopped onion

½ cup finely chopped celery

¼ cup chopped Italian parsley, plus extra for garnish

2 tsp Old Bay seasoning

Grated zest of ½ lemon

Salt and black pepper

1 lb cooked and peeled crawfish tails, rinsed

4 lobster roll buns (or other white buns)

Butter, as needed

Crawfish Rolls

SERVES 2 TO 4 The crawfish roll was created impromptu. "I was looking for a way to feature seafood on our daily menu, but I wasn't crazy about po'boys," reveals chef Ryan Savoie. "In this part of the country, people live and die by their ideas of what makes a good po'boy, and I'd just as soon stay out of that dialogue. So I set my sights on the delicious lobster roll and decided to use crawfish."

In a large bowl, combine mayonnaise, onion, celery, parsley, Old Bay seasoning, and lemon zest. Season with salt and pepper. Add crawfish and mix well. Cover and refrigerate for at least 2 hours.

Slice rolls lengthwise to create a deep slit. Butter the outsides of the buns. Heat a frying pan over medium-high heat. Toast buns in the pan for 1 minute on each side or until crispy and golden.

Spoon the crawfish mixture into the buns, garnish with parsley, and serve immediately.

Shun Japanese Kitchen

NAOKI YOSHIDA

★ After eighteen years as sushi chef at Nippon (the Japanese restaurant founded by his parents in 1986), Naoki Yoshida opened his own restaurant concept, Shun, in fall of 2018 to bridge his Japanese heritage and Houston upbringing. Passionate about cultivating Japanese cuisine, Yoshida regards his restaurant as a "second-generation Japanese kitchen," where ingredients come both from local farmers and fishers and from Japan. In fact, Shun, named after a Japanese word that translates as "the peak of the season," features a new menu every three months, to showcase the best of each season.

Yoshida wants his guests to feel invited, as if they came to his home. The *noren*, the customary entrance drapes in Shun's house orange color, represents the flair and young fire that drives their Japanese kitchen. Bold murals line the reception hall, and the inviting dining room, with its warm, natural tones, is augmented with personal touches such as macramé art made by wife and co-owner, Renée. The sake trays allow patrons to pick a cup and sip one of over sixty varieties of sake. "Personalization is the Japanese way," explains Yoshida. He put his own craftsmanship into the wooden sushi and sake bar tops that he fitted and finished himself.

Everything here is made in-house, including condiments like pickled ginger, chili oil, and soy sauce. And since unagi is an unsustainable choice these days, Yoshida prepares *anago*, a saltwater eel that he fillets, smokes, and seasons. Inspired dishes—think crab-and-shiitake tortellini with uni (sea urchin) beurre blanc; a hot pot rich with house-made fish cake and Creole shrimp ball; and wagyu steak with miso brown butter and kabocha purée—skillfully marry local and traditional culinary traditions. At Shun, we truly savor Japanese cuisine with local inspiration.

Poke mix

½ small white or
  red onion, thinly sliced

½ cucumber, halved
  lengthwise and thinly
  sliced

½ large watermelon
  radish or any seasonal
  radish, quartered and
  thinly sliced

1 lb skinless sashimi-
  grade salmon, cut into
  ¾-inch cubes

1 pack dried instant
  noodles (optional)

Shichimi, for sprinkling

Chili threads, for garnish

Sauce

1 cup soy sauce

½ cup chili oil

½ Tbsp shichimi
  (Japanese chili powder)

1 tsp grated ginger

½ tsp Sriracha

Hanabi Poke

SERVES 4 Poke in its most traditional form is cubes of raw fish seasoned in a sauce. Naoki Yoshida's version, which won first place in the Houston poke showdown hosted by Houston Press in 2017, combines Hawaiian tradition and a touch of Houston heat.

Be sure to cut all the vegetables to the same thickness to create consistency of texture. The poke can also be served as a main with steamed rice and crunchy cucumber salad.

Poke mix Have the vegetables and salmon ready for assembly. In a small bowl, crush the noodles, if using, and set aside.

Sauce In a bowl, combine all ingredients.

Assembly In a bowl, mix together the sauce and salmon. Place salmon in a line on a serving plate. Garnish with vegetables, dried noodles, if using, and shichimi and chili threads.

2 (12-oz) fresh skin-on
  Gulf snapper fillets

2 tsp kosher salt

2 Tbsp sake

¼ cup white miso

¼ cup mirin (sweet sake)

½ tsp local honey, plus
  extra to taste

Steamed rice, for serving

Miso Snappy

SERVES 4 This wonderfully straightforward recipe applies a traditional Japanese curing method to local snapper. After a quick bath in sake, the fish is simply immersed in a mixture of local raw honey, mirin, and white miso until it is thoroughly infused with sweet and salty notes. The longer you leave it in the marinade, the deeper the flavor. Partner it with store-bought seaweed salad, sliced cucumber, and steamed rice and that's dinner done!

Cut each fillet in half. Sprinkle salt on each piece of fish and place them in a shallow bowl of sake for 15 minutes. Rinse off sake and pat dry the fish with paper towel. (The process releases any unwanted moisture, to prevent the fish from spoiling during the curing process.)

In a blender, combine miso, mirin, and honey. Place fish in a sealable container, pour over the marinade, cover, and refrigerate for at least 24 hours and up to 3 days.

Preheat oven to 375°F.

Rinse off miso from the fish. (If left on, the thick paste will burn before the fish is fully cooked.) Place fish, skin-side up, on a baking sheet and bake for 15 minutes. (Do not move the fish or it will fall apart.) Using a spatula, carefully transfer fish to a serving plate and serve immediately with rice.

Sparrow Cookshop

MONICA POPE

⭐ Monica Pope has been a pioneering presence on Houston's dining scene since 1992, when she opened her first restaurant, The Quilted Toque. Pope spearheaded the farm-to-table movement in Houston more than twenty years ago, spending the better part of her life as a chef preaching *and* practicing her trademarked food philosophy "Eat where your food lives." Those in the know bag a table at her regular pop-up dinners.

There's not a local vegetable she hasn't cooked with. Yet it wouldn't be accurate to regard Pope solely as a vegetable-driven chef, when's she more than capable of delivering hearty meaty fare. Think elk Bolognese, wild boar tenderloin, lamb fries, and whole-roasted hog. For Pope, nose-to-tail cooking is not a trend; it is simply how she cooks.

Sparrow Cookshop is her work/live studio, where she teaches cooking classes, hosts monthly Sunday Suppers, and has special events such as a bycatch dinner with local fishers and the Gulf Restoration Network. "I have one long table, where we are all connected and nobody is excluded," says Pope, who also volunteers her time and energy to local charities like Recipe for Success, which brings awareness to childhood obesity, and I'll Have What She's Having, which raises awareness of women's wellness.

In late 2018, Pope and her business partner, Adam Brackman, launched Decatur Bar and Popup Factory at 2310 Decatur. The restaurant features a rotating chef series, overseen by Pope, who guides the resident chefs. "It's a place to gather, connect, and commit to building personal and professional infrastructures," she says. As a fierce champion of our local community, Pope is one of Houston's standout culinary heroes.

▶ **Charred Eggplant and Okra with Burrata** | p. 198

1 large eggplant

Kosher or sea salt

3 Tbsp good-quality olive oil (divided)

15 okras, cut diagonally into 1-inch pieces

1 Tbsp good-quality shoyu (preferably Haku Sakura Cherry Blossom Shoyu)

1 Tbsp roasted rice wine vinegar

1 whole burrata

1 Tbsp fennel pollen

1 tsp moringa powder (see headnote)

Handful of tarragon leaves

2 Tbsp extra-virgin olive oil

Charred Eggplant and Okra with Burrata

SERVES 4 Summers in Houston are all about okra and eggplant, two crops that thrive in the heat. Chef Monica Pope encourages you to be creative with seasonal bounty and use an assortment of vegetables from your garden or the farmers' market. Pope sources moringa powder from Finca Tres Robles, but you can find it in health stores as well.

Cherry blossom shoyu is a light soy sauce infused with pickled flowers. When combined with roasted rice wine vinegar, it makes an exquisite dressing for this charred vegetable salad.

Halve the eggplant lengthwise. Using a sharp knife, score the flesh in 4 or 5 spots. Season generously with salt.

Heat 2 tablespoons olive oil in a large frying pan over high heat. Add eggplants and sear for 1 minute on each side. Reduce heat to medium and cook for 10 to 15 minutes, until softened and charred. Transfer eggplants, flesh-side down, to a plate and let cool.

Heat ½ tablespoon oil in the frying pan over high heat. Add half the okra (to avoid overcrowding) and sauté for 3 to 4 minutes, until charred and tender. Season with salt and transfer to a baking sheet. Heat the remaining ½ tablespoon oil in the pan and repeat with the remaining okra.

Cut eggplants diagonally into slices 1 to 1½ inches thick. In a large bowl, gently mix eggplant with okra. Add shoyu and vinegar and toss lightly.

Arrange mixture in a half circle in a decorative bowl. Place burrata in the center. Sprinkle fennel pollen, moringa powder, and tarragon over vegetables and drizzle extra-virgin olive oil overtop.

3 Tbsp olive oil, for frying (divided)

3 shallots, thinly sliced

3 cups heavy cream

2 to 3 sprigs thyme

1 Tbsp local raw honey

Kosher or sea salt

1 tsp lemon juice, plus extra to taste

2 lbs assorted summer squash

Handful of tarragon leaves, for garnish

1 Tbsp extra-virgin olive oil, for drizzling

Summer Squash in Honey-Shallot Cream Sauce

SERVES 4 TO 6 When you join a farm-share or community-supported agriculture (CSA), you never know quite what you'll find in your share until you lay out the week's harvest on the kitchen table. But with this versatile honey-shallot cream sauce in your repertoire, you'll find it much easier to use up any harvest surprises—it pairs well with almost every vegetable, from peas, pole beans, and leeks to wintry sprouts, rainbow carrots, and chards.

Heat 1 tablespoon oil in a large saucepan over medium heat. Add shallots and sauté for 5 minutes or until softened. Add cream and bring to a boil. Reduce heat to medium-low, add thyme and honey, and simmer gently for 15 to 20 minutes, until reduced by a quarter. (Reduce heat if necessary to maintain the simmer.) Season with salt and lemon juice.

Cut the summer squash to the same size, keeping smaller ones whole.

Heat 1 tablespoon oil in a frying pan over high heat. Add half the squash (to avoid overcrowding) and sear for 3 minutes or until softened and charred. Season with salt and transfer to a large plate. Heat the remaining 1 tablespoon oil in the pan and repeat with the remaining squash.

Add squash to the cream sauce and gently spoon through, taking care not to break or damage them. Pour into a serving bowl. Garnish with tarragon and finish with a drizzle of extra-virgin olive oil and a squeeze of lemon juice.

SweetCup Gelato & Sorbet Originale

JASMINE CHIDA

⭐ Here's the scoop: SweetCup is serving up seriously good ice cream across the city—all because of Jasmine Chida.

Chida had a solid start by studying the art of frozen desserts at the Carpigiani Gelato University in Bologna, Italy. She was destined to churn out an exciting range of flavors, thanks in large part to her upbringing. This Texas-born gelato artisan draws much of her inspiration from her childhood in San Antonio, her Greek-Persian heritage, and even flavor profiles from her husband's homeland of India. Her pomegranate-rose sorbet is a nod to the flavors of the Middle East, while a toasted black sesame gelato is a nostalgic tribute to the snacks packed in her lunchboxes when she was a child. The most distinguished flavors are unconventional and quirky but thoroughly grown-up and always delicious. Crowd favorites include the chocolatey Texas sheet cake gelato, vanilla bean tres leches, and Texan kulfi, an Indian ice cream made with pecans praline, cardamom cream, and bourbon. "I am constantly trying to innovate, and to evolve SweetCup as a better version of what it was yesterday."

SweetCup opened shop in 2012 in the Montrose District, followed by an outpost in Oak Forest/Garden Oaks in 2017. By the end of 2018, SweetCup was available at every Whole Foods across the city, all Central Market stores across the state, and selected Marriott hotels and restaurants, expanding with a wholesale commissary kitchen in 2019.

And the story behind the company name? Chida named her business after a cherished family memory. It's what her dad always said when they went out for ice cream: "Come, let's get a sweet cup."

▶ **Dirty Coconut Sorbet** | p. 203
Panna Cotta–Lemon Curd Gelato | p. 204–5

3 (13.5-oz) cans full-fat
  coconut milk
¾ cup crystallized sugar
½ cup semi-sweet
  chocolate chips
1 Tbsp organic coconut oil

Dirty Coconut Sorbet

MAKES 1½ QUARTS Many of Jasmine Chida's flavors have a backstory. Before she opened her business, Chida and her husband went to Hawaii and discovered coconut chocolate pie: delicious layers of coconut cream and dark chocolate on a graham cracker base. Her vegan-friendly sorbet here sees lacings of crunchy chocolate in creamy coconut sorbet.

A day in advance, put the container of your ice-cream maker in the freezer.

Put a 2-quart metal loaf pan (or freezer-safe container) in the freezer to chill for at least 1 hour.

Pour coconut milk into a saucepan. Add sugar and whisk for 1 minute. Bring mixture to a gentle simmer over medium-low heat and stir continuously for 1 minute. Transfer to a large glass bowl or container and let cool completely.

Cover and chill mixture in the refrigerator for 1 hour. (Mixture must be completely cooled before it's poured into the ice-cream maker.)

Remove mixture from the refrigerator and stir. Pour it into the ice-cream maker and churn for 15 to 25 minutes, until mixture has become soft ice cream.

Meanwhile, melt chocolate chips and coconut oil in a small saucepan over medium-low heat. Drizzle chocolate sauce into the sorbet and churn for 5 minutes.

Transfer the sorbet from the ice-cream maker to the loaf pan. Cover and freeze in the coldest part of your freezer for at least 2 hours. To serve, scoop out as needed!

Gelato

4 egg yolks

¾ cup pure cane sugar

2 cups whole milk

1 cup heavy cream

Panna Cotta–Lemon Curd Gelato

MAKES 2 QUARTS Dip a spoon in this gelato, discover the layers of bright yet creamy flavors, and know that happiness is but a lick away. This popular and versatile gelato can be made throughout the seasons: use Meyer lemons in winter or limes in summer for a different citrus flavor.

Gelato A day in advance, put the container of your ice-cream maker in the freezer.

Put a 2-quart metal loaf pan (or freezer-safe container) in the freezer to chill for at least 1 hour.

In a bowl, beat egg yolks and sugar until pale and fluffy.

Heat milk and cream in a large saucepan over medium heat, stirring frequently, until texture becomes frothy and just begins to boil.

Slowly pour the hot cream mixture, a little at a time, into egg mixture, stirring continuously for 1 minute. Pour mixture into the saucepan. To prevent it from curdling, reduce heat to low and stir for another minute or until mixture thickens enough to coat the back of a spoon. (If the mixture does curdle and you catch it early on, fill a large bowl with ice-cold water, place the saucepan in the bowl, and stir continuously. Then strain through a fine-mesh sieve into a bowl.) Pour mixture into a clean bowl and let cool completely.

Cover and refrigerate for 1 hour or until completely chilled. (Mixture must be completely cooled before it's poured into the ice-cream maker.)

Remove mixture from the refrigerator and stir. Pour it into the ice-cream maker and churn for 20 to 30 minutes, until mixture has become soft ice cream.

Transfer the gelato from the ice-cream maker to a freezer-safe container. Cover and freeze until needed.

Lemon curd

½ cup pure cane sugar

3 egg yolks

2 Tbsp grated lemon zest

½ cup (1 stick) salted
   butter, softened

½ cup lemon juice
   (see Note)

1 Tbsp pure vanilla extract
   or ½ vanilla bean

1 Tbsp cornstarch

Lemon slices, for garnish

Lemon curd In a large bowl, whisk together sugar and egg yolks until pale and foamy. Add lemon zest while whisking.

Transfer mixture to a saucepan and heat over low heat, stirring continuously, until hot but not boiling. Add butter and stir to fully incorporate. Add lemon juice and vanilla extract (or scrape in the seeds of the vanilla bean) and stir for 1 minute.

In a small bowl, combine cornstarch and 1 tablespoon cold water. Add mixture to the pan and stir over medium heat until thickened. Strain mixture through a fine-mesh sieve into a bowl and let cool completely, then cover and chill in the refrigerator for 1 hour.

Assembly Scoop a third of the gelato into the chilled loaf pan (or container). Using a spatula, spread it out in an even layer. Spread a thin layer of lemon curd on top (like jam on toast). Repeat and build layers of gelato and lemon curd until you have 3 to 4 layers of each.

Drizzle remaining lemon curd on top, cover, and freeze in the coldest part of your freezer for 6 to 8 hours. To serve the gelato as dessert, remove the loaf pan from the freezer and tip over onto a serving platter to let the gelato drop out. Garnish with lemon slices. Alternatively, scoop the gelato as needed from the pan.

The Tasting Room

BETO GUTIERREZ

⭐ Wine bar fans had this one on their radar as soon as it opened in 2003. In a leafy corner spot in Uptown Park, the Tasting Room is perfect for what the name suggests: tasting wine. Whether it is with a group of friends at one of the wooden communal tables or a tête-à-tête outside on the patio, there's ample choice of wines by the glass or bottle. Over the years, the food menu was developed to meet the demands of the wine bar's growing clientele. You can order traditional cheese boards, roasted nuts, and marinated olives, but shareables like charred octopus with crispy-fried spiced potatoes and aioli, and roasted Brussels sprouts tossed with duck confit and pine nuts elevate it from the typical wine-bar menu. In fact, today's food menu warrants a visit, even without considering the vino—*almost*. After all, even that lunchtime smoked salmon tartine or the salad with the candied pecans and goat cheese calls out for a nice pairing. It's no surprise that the Tasting Room opened a second location in CityCentre in 2011.

Chef Beto Gutierrez, who joined Lasco Enterprises (the hospitality group behind the Tasting Room) in 2015, is used to running the kitchen for both the wine bar's regular menu and private events. He comes from a hotel background, having worked at the historic boutique hotel La Posada in his hometown of Laredo. "The difference is that I don't have to worry about guests calling for room service at six in the morning," he says, laughing. "I'm glad to be here with a small restaurant group, where I can really flourish."

▶ **Rib-Eye Tacos with Avocado-Tomatillo Salsa** | p. 208

Steak tacos

1 Tbsp kosher salt

1 Tbsp black pepper

1 Tbsp paprika

1 Tbsp garlic powder

1 Tbsp onion powder

2 (14- to 16-oz) well-marbled prime rib eye

Avocado-tomatillo salsa

5 large tomatillos, husks removed and chopped

2 to 4 serrano peppers, stemmed and seeded

¼ white onion, finely chopped

4 cloves garlic, finely chopped

2 tsp kosher salt

1 ripe avocado, peeled, pitted, and chopped

½ bunch cilantro, plus a handful for garnish

Assembly

5 to 6 jalapeño peppers

10 to 12 tortillas (preferably butter flour tortillas)

½ white onion, thinly sliced

3 to 4 lime wedges

Cilantro leaves

Roasted red bell peppers, cut into strips (optional)

Rib-Eye Tacos with Avocado-Tomatillo Salsa

SERVES 5 TO 6 PEOPLE Chef Beto Gutierrez, who grew up in meat-centric South Texas, knows how to grill a good rib eye and shares here how it's done. A grilled steak loves a little serrano heat, tomatillo tartness, and avocado creaminess, and this recipe rolls all of that into one taco. For the barbecue, the chef uses a ⁵⁰⁄₅₀ blend of oak and mesquite charcoal, but feel free to experiment.

Steak tacos In a small bowl, combine salt, pepper, paprika, and garlic and onion powders. Rub seasoning on both sides of the steaks. Place steaks on a plate, cover with a dish towel, and refrigerate for up to 30 minutes.

Avocado-tomatillo salsa In a blender, purée all ingredients except cilantro for 30 seconds or until smooth. Add cilantro and pulse until cilantro is coarsely mixed in.

Assembly Preheat a grill over high heat. If using an outdoor grill, open all the grill vents.

Place steaks on the grill and grill for 5 to 6 minutes on each side, keeping the lid closed. (To get nice grill marks, rotate each steak 45 degrees after the first 3 minutes on each side.) On the same grill, add jalapeños and char for 2 minutes or until softened and blistered. Set aside. Transfer steaks to a plate and let rest for 10 minutes.

Meanwhile, warm tortillas for 30 seconds on the hot grill, then keep warm in a tortilla warmer (or wrap in a dish towel on a plate).

Slice the steaks against the grain into ¼-inch-thick slices. Arrange on a serving platter and garnish with the grilled jalapeños, onion, lime, cilantro, and roasted peppers, if using. Serve with a bowl of salsa and warm tortillas.

Polenta

1 cup heavy cream

3 cups chicken stock

1 cup dry polenta

½ cup chopped pecans

½ cup grated Parmesan

1 Tbsp thyme leaves

1 Tbsp chopped Italian parsley

Salt

Pear-bourbon sauce

1 Tbsp butter

4 small shallots, finely chopped

2 Bosc or D'Anjou pears, peeled, cored, and cut into ½-inch cubes (divided)

1 cup chicken stock

¼ cup bourbon

¼ cup apple cider vinegar

¼ cup honey

2 Tbsp molasses

Salt and black pepper

Greens

1 Tbsp olive oil

2 cloves garlic, sliced

4 slices bacon, cooked and chopped

Bunch of kale, stems removed and leaves chopped

¼ cup white wine

1 tsp Dijon mustard

Salt and black pepper

Assembly

8 semi-boneless Texas quail

Salt and black pepper

2 Tbsp cold butter, cut into ½-inch cubes

2 Tbsp grated Parmesan, for garnish

Grilled Quail, Pecan Polenta, and Pear-Bourbon Sauce

SERVES 4 Talk about flavors of Texas! This ensemble of grilled quail, warm fruity sauce, and pecan-studded polenta is rib-sticking delicious. Also, a multitasker can have this on the table in 40 minutes. Find quail in the freezer section of most supermarkets.

Polenta Bring cream and stock to a boil in a medium saucepan over medium-high heat. Gradually whisk in the polenta in a steady stream, then reduce heat to low and stir for 6 to 7 minutes, until polenta is soft and thick. Fold in pecans, Parmesan, thyme, and parsley. Season with salt, cover, and remove from heat. Set aside.

Pear-bourbon sauce Melt butter in a small saucepan over medium-low heat. Add shallots and half the pears and sauté for 10 minutes or until caramelized. Remove pan from heat and stir in stock, bourbon, vinegar, honey, and molasses. Return the pan to the stove and bring to a boil. Reduce heat to low and simmer for 5 minutes. Remove from heat and let sit for at least 5 minutes.

Transfer mixture to a blender. Since the mixture is hot, remove the center cap from the blender lid and cover the hole with a dish towel so steam can escape. Blend until smooth. Return to the saucepan, add the remaining half of the pear, and season with salt and pepper. Keep warm.

Greens Heat oil in a small frying pan over medium heat. Add garlic and sauté for 30 seconds. Add bacon and kale and cook for 1 minute. Pour in wine and cook for another 5 minutes or until the kale is softened and tender.

Turn off the heat and stir in mustard. Season with salt and pepper and set aside.

Assembly Heat a grill over medium heat. Season quail with salt and pepper, and grill for 3 to 4 minutes on each side. Set aside but keep warm. Whisk butter into the pear-bourbon sauce.

Distribute polenta over four plates and top with greens. Spoon the sauce around the polenta, place 2 quails on each plate, and garnish with Parmesan. Serve immediately.

Theodore Rex

JUSTIN YU

Today, the Warehouse District is evolving as a cultural hub, home to a bevy of art galleries, music venues—and one of the best restaurants in town. Back in 2012, when Justin Yu opened his first restaurant, Oxheart, the area largely comprised dilapidated industrial buildings. But Yu drew a steady flock of food lovers to the neighborhood and undeniably put it on the map. Set up for success, it could easily have gone on had Yu not found himself in need of a change. In 2017, Yu closed Oxheart, the tasting-menu restaurant that earned him a James Beard Award, and reopened in the same spot six months later with Theodore Rex.

T. Rex, as it was almost immediately called, has all the attributes of a modern bistro, from the menu driven by local and seasonal ingredients to the laid-back ambiance of its intimate, twenty-eight-seat locale. The style is casual-industrial, with informal-dining details such as the drawers at each table that hold all your silverware. What makes it exceptional is the chef's undefinable *sui generis* cuisine. Each articulated dish has its own narrative: handpicked ingredients are meticulously prepared and skillfully put together. It's why a dish like tomato toast has food tongues wagging; a comfort-food rice porridge can transform into an unforgettable dish; and purple thyme–speckled tangelo supremes make us wish it was citrus season year-round. The dishes seem deceptively simple, at times even rustic, until you take the first bite and your palate awakens to the most intriguing of flavors and exciting textures.

And while Yu certainly helms the restaurant, its operation involves teamwork. Theodore Rex is run in large part by Yu's restaurant family—the same team that ran Oxheart, responsible for the feel-at-home service, the gem-rich wine list, and, quite frankly, the fun vibe.

▶ **Smoked Gulf Fish Spread** | p. 213

Pickled grapes

¼ cup white distilled vinegar

¾ cup champagne vinegar

½ cup granulated sugar

3 cloves

1 star anise

50 green grapes

Simple syrup

1 cup granulated sugar

Grape Expectations

- Muscadine grapes (see headnote)

1¼ oz vodka (preferably Reyka)

½ oz lemon juice

½ oz Simple Syrup (see here)

¼ oz crème de violette

1 pickled grape

Grape Expectations Cocktail

SERVES 1 Chef Justin Yu sources grapes for this seasonal cocktail from Pomona Farms in Blanco, Texas. Muscadine are dark, nearly black grapes with a thick, tough skins and are popular in the summer and early fall, when they grow wild along the Buffalo Bayou. If you cannot find Muscadine grapes, substitute with Concord or red grapes (in that order).

Pickled grapes In a small saucepan, combine both vinegars, sugar, cloves, star anise, and 1 cup water and heat over medium heat until sugar is dissolved. Let pickling liquid cool to room temperature. Remove the spices.

Put grapes into a sterilized 1-quart canning jar. Pour in pickling liquid, filling to the top. Place a piece of cheesecloth on top and press the grapes into the liquid. Screw the lid on tightly. Store in a refrigerator for 1 week before using.

Simple syrup In a saucepan, combine sugar and 1 cup water and heat through until sugar is dissolved. Set aside to cool to room temperature. Refrigerate until needed.

Grape Expectations Place a coupe glass in the refrigerator or freezer to chill.

In a cocktail shaker, muddle Muscadine grapes. Add the remaining ingredients except pickled grape and add a scoop of crushed ice to fill the shaker halfway. Shake for 1 minute or until the liquid is cold.

Fill the chilled coupe glass to the top with crushed ice. Using a sieve, fine-strain the cocktail into the coupe and garnish with a pickled grape.

Note: The pickled grapes are also delicious in a crispy salad with pecans and crumbly feta, on a cheese board, or simply on their own as a snack.

Smoked fish

1 (1½- to 2-lb) whole snapper or other white-fleshed Gulf fish, cleaned

Kosher salt

Apple or cherry wood chips, for smoking

Fish spread

1 egg yolk

1 small clove garlic, finely chopped

2 Tbsp Dijon mustard

1 cup vegetable oil

½ Tbsp sherry vinegar

Salt and black pepper

Smoked Fish (see here)

Assembly

Pickles, edible flowers, microgreens, and seasonal radishes, for garnish

Seeded crackers and/or crusty bread

Smoked Gulf Fish Spread

SERVES 4 TO 6 (AS AN APPETIZER) Chef Justin Yu's smoked fish spread need not come with an expiration date; it will be gone long before that. The recipe requires smoked fish, which can be easily prepared at home with a stovetop smoker, on the barbecue, or in a backyard smoker. If you don't feel like smoking fish, whole smoked mackerel (available at Phoenicia Specialty Foods) also works well.

Smoked fish Pat dry the fish with paper towel, then season with salt.

To smoke the fish in a stovetop smoker, place 2 tablespoons wood chips in the bottom pan and place the tray on top. Cover with foil (for easy cleanup) and place the fish on top. Cover the pan and smoke over medium heat for 20 minutes.

Take the pan outside and open (to prevent the smoke from filling your kitchen). Set aside to cool.

Remove the skin, then pick the fish off the bones and put it into a bowl. Using your fingers, separate the fish and discard any bones (see Note).

Fish spread Put egg yolk, garlic, mustard, and 1 tablespoon ice-cold water into a bowl and whisk for 30 seconds or until foamy. Continuing to whisk, slowly pour in the oil until emulsified. Whisk in vinegar, a little at a time. Season with salt and pepper. (The mayonnaise can be stored in an airtight container in the refrigerator for up to 1 week.)

Put fish into a bowl and stir in mayonnaise in batches, a spoonful at a time, until mixture is smooth and spreadable.

Assembly Load the fish spread into a piping bag. Pipe into 2 (¼-pint) mason jars and smooth the top with the back of a spoon or a damp paper towel. Garnish with pickles, edible flowers, microgreens, and seasonal radishes. Serve on a plate surrounded by seeded crackers (and/or crusty bread).

Note: The head and bones make a terrific smoky fish stock.

TRIBUTE at
The Houstonian

NEAL COX

★ When the sun sets at The Houstonian Hotel, Club & Spa, the magnificent Live Oak is lit with thousands of fairy lights, putting everyone in a celebratory mood. The twenty-seven acres of wooded grounds are an oasis of tranquility in the heart of the hustling and bustling Galleria area.

The Houstonian is renowned for its Texas-style grandeur, and TRIBUTE was but an extension of that opulence when it opened in 2018. It has a stunning entrance wall of back-lit wine lockers, a wall of glass windows overlooking the gardens, and a private room stocked with 4,000 bottles of wine. Moreover, executive chef Neal Cox brings together flavors that in so many ways define Houston's cuisine, intertwining culinary traditions of Texas, Louisiana, and Mexico—which he affectionately dubs "Tex-Lex." He explains, "We're influenced by great cooking all around us, but we're inspired by regional recipes and the authentic dishes that have been passed on by our own families and the many great cooks before us."

The well-articulated menu champions the wonderful flavors of the region: Gulf oysters punctuated with Mexican chorizo butter (page 217), seared duck over rich Louisiana "dirty" rice, slowly braised cabrito (kid goat), and wild boar empanadas—all these dishes embrace local food cultures. And so the moniker really could not be more apt: Cox's Tex-Lex cuisine is an unapologetic tribute to Southeast Texas cooking.

▶ **Smoked Beef Ribs with Grilled Creamed Corn** | p. 218–19

Chorizo butter

2 anchovy fillets, finely chopped

1 cup Mexican chorizo, cooked and fat drained

¾ cup (1½ sticks) butter, room temperature

¼ cup chopped garlic

1 Tbsp chili flakes

1 Tbsp finely chopped Italian parsley

1 Tbsp finely chopped cilantro

1 Tbsp lemon juice

1 tsp fine table salt

Oysters

12 Gulf oysters, shucked on the half shell

¾ cup Chorizo Butter (see here), room temperature

1 cup grated Parmesan

Crusty bread, sliced, to serve

Wood-Grilled Oysters with Mexican Chorizo Sauce

SERVES 4 These wood-grilled oysters bubbling with chorizo butter are a Tex-Lex delight. Even better, if you prepare the chorizo butter a day in advance, the oysters will whip up as quick as a wink. Mexican-style chorizo is a ground pork sausage boosted with spices such as smoked paprika and chili. When preparing oysters for grilling, Chef Cox avoids adding too many ingredients, which can mask the delicate flavors of the oysters.

Chorizo butter In a stand mixer fitted with the paddle attachment, mix together all ingredients on low speed until incorporated. Increase speed to medium and mix for another 3 minutes. Set aside at room temperature or refrigerate until needed.

Oysters Start a wood or lump charcoal fire in your grill and preheat until fire has burned downed and coals are hot. Place oysters on a grill rack directly over the coals and grill for 2 minutes or until edges of the oysters start to curl. Spoon a tablespoon of chorizo butter on top of each oyster and cook, covered, for another 2 minutes.

Sprinkle Parmesan on each oyster and remove from the grill. Serve immediately with crusty bread.

Beef ribs

1 cup barbecue beef rub
(preferably TRIBUTE
Texas Dry Rub)

1 (4-bone) rack beef plate
ribs (preferably Prime
or wagyu)

Creamed corn

4 ears corn

3 Tbsp olive oil (divided)

Kosher salt and black
pepper

1 cup heavy cream

½ cup smoked bacon,
finely chopped

1 small yellow onion,
finely chopped

1 clove garlic, finely
chopped

1 Tbsp all-purpose flour

½ cup grated Parmesan,
plus extra for finishing

2 Tbsp hot sauce
(preferably Valentina)

Chopped Italian parsley,
for finishing

Smoked Beef Ribs with Grilled Creamed Corn

SERVES 4 These juicy smoked ribs are fall-off-the-bone tender. Pickled vegetables, such as Mexican-style vegetable escabeche, add enough sharpness to balance out the dish and cut through the richness of the creamed corn and ribs.

Beef ribs Generously rub the barbecue seasoning all over the ribs and set aside at room temperature for 2 hours.

Preheat a smoker or wood-burning grill (Chef Cox advises to use oak, pecan, or hickory wood) to a temperature of 275°F. Place a small pan of water inside your cooker to keep it humid.

Place ribs on the grill rack and cover. Adjust the air damper accordingly to maintain constant temperature. Cook for 5 hours or until meat is tender but not falling off the bone and the internal temperature is 200°F. Transfer ribs to a plate and let rest for at least 30 minutes.

Creamed corn Remove husk from the corn. Rub 2 tablespoons oil over the corn, then season with salt and pepper. Let sit for 20 minutes.

Grill corn over a wood or charcoal fire for 5 minutes or until charred. (Do not overcook or the corn will lose its sweet flavor.) Transfer to a plate and let cool.

Using a sharp knife, stand an ear up on a cutting board and carefully shave off the kernels. Take care not to cut too close to the cob itself, as you don't want the tougher membrane mixed in with the kernels.

Using the back of a knife, scrape the exposed cobs into a separate bowl and extract as much of the natural liquid as possible. Whisk in cream, then set aside.

Heat the remaining 1 tablespoon oil in a frying pan over medium heat. Add bacon and cook for 3 minutes or until slightly crisp. Add onion and cook for another 5 minutes or until onion is softened and translucent. Add garlic and sauté for 1 minute, stirring continuously, to prevent onion and garlic from burning or caramelizing. Add corn and cook for 1 minute. Season with salt and pepper.

Assembly
Sliced jalapeños, shaved
    carrots, pickled onions,
    and fresh cilantro, for
    garnish

Stir in the flour until thoroughly combined.
Pour in the cream mixture and simmer for
5 minutes, stirring occasionally. Adjust heat as
necessary.

Transfer 1 cup of the mixture to a blender and
purée. With the motor still running, add Parmesan
and hot sauce and blend for 30 seconds.

Pour mixture back into the pan, stir to combine,
and cook for 5 minutes on low heat. Remove from
heat and season with salt and pepper.

Assembly Cut between the rib bones and portion
on individual plates, or serve family-style on a
platter. Garnish with jalapeños, carrots, pickled
onions, and cilantro. Spoon creamed corn onto
each plate and finish with Parmesan and parsley.

Metric Conversion Chart

VOLUME

Imperial or U.S.	Metric
⅛ tsp	0.5 ml
¼ tsp	1 ml
½ tsp	2.5 ml
¾ tsp	4 ml
1 tsp	5 ml
½ Tbsp	8 ml
1 Tbsp	15 ml
1½ Tbsp	23 ml
2 Tbsp	30 ml
¼ cup	60 ml
⅓ cup	80 ml
½ cup	125 ml
⅔ cup	165 ml
¾ cup	185 ml
1 cup	250 ml
1¼ cups	310 ml
1⅓ cups	330 ml
1½ cups	375 ml
1⅔ cups	415 ml
1¾ cups	435 ml
2 cups	500 ml
2¼ cups	560 ml
2⅓ cups	580 ml
2½ cups	625 ml
2¾ cups	690 ml
3 cups	750 ml
4 cups/1 qt	1 L
5 cups	1.25 L
6 cups	1.5 L
7 cups	1.75 L
8 cups/2 qts	2 L

WEIGHT

Imperial or U.S.	Metric
½ oz	15 g
1 oz	30 g
2 oz	60 g
3 oz	85 g
4 oz (¼ lb)	115 g
5 oz	140 g
6 oz	170 g
7 oz	200 g
8 oz (½ lb)	225 g
9 oz	255 g
10 oz	285 g
11 oz	310 g
12 oz (¾ lb)	340 g
13 oz	370 g
14 oz	400 g
15 oz	425 g
16 oz (1 lb)	450 g
1¼ lbs	570 g
1½ lbs	670 g
2 lbs	900 g
3 lbs	1.4 kg
4 lbs	1.8 kg
5 lbs	2.3 kg
6 lbs	2.7 kg

LIQUID MEASURES
(for alcohol)

Imperial or U.S.	Metric
1 fl oz	30 ml
2 fl oz	60 ml
3 fl oz	90 ml
4 fl oz	120 ml

CANS AND JARS

Imperial or U.S.	Metric
14 oz	398 ml
28 oz	796 ml

LINEAR

Imperial or U.S.	Metric
⅛ inch	3 mm
¼ inch	6 mm
½ inch	12 mm
¾ inch	2 cm
1 inch	2.5 cm
1¼ inches	3 cm
1½ inches	3.5 cm
1¾ inches	4.5 cm
2 inches	5 cm
2½ inches	6.5 cm
3 inches	7.5 cm
4 inches	10 cm
5 inches	12.5 cm
6 inches	15 cm
7 inches	18 cm
8 inches	20 cm
9 inches	23 cm
10 inches	25 cm
11 inches	28 cm
12 inches (1 foot)	30 cm
13 inches	33 cm
18 inches	46 cm

TEMPERATURE
(for oven temperatures, see chart at right)

Imperial or U.S.	Metric
90°F	32°C
120°F	49°C
125°F	52°C
130°F	54°C
135°F	57°C
140°F	60°C
145°F	63°C
150°F	66°C
155°F	68°C
160°F	71°C
165°F	74°C
170°F	77°C
175°F	80°C
180°F	82°C
185°F	85°C
190°F	88°C
195°F	91°C
200°F	93°C
225°F	107°C
250°F	121°C
275°F	135°C
300°F	149°C
325°F	163°C
350°F	177°C
360°F	182°C
375°F	191°C

OVEN TEMPERATURE

Imperial or U.S.	Metric
200°F	95°C
250°F	120°C
275°F	135°C
300°F	150°C
325°F	160°C
350°F	180°C
375°F	190°C
400°F	200°C
425°F	220°C
450°F	230°C

BAKING PANS

Imperial or U.S.	Metric
5- × 9-inch loaf pan	2 L loaf pan
9- × 13-inch cake pan	4 L cake pan
13- × 18-inch baking sheet	33 × 46 cm baking sheet

Acknowledgments

★ ★ ★

This book was put together a year after Hurricane Harvey all but destroyed the city. The city was paralyzed for weeks, in some areas for months, and cleanup was hampered by the sheer scale of destruction. My heart leapt when the industry got together to cook for those who needed it and to support their peers. I myself became a flooding statistic on August 28, 2017, when our house took four feet of bayou water and forced us into a rescue boat with the Cajun Navy. Community spirit is what makes #HoustonStrong, and I want to acknowledge that here.

This book could not have come about without the support of many people. First and foremost, I'd like to thank all the chefs who shared their stories, their recipes, and their insights. I'll cherish that forever. Chefs have arduous hours—they can work 12-hour shifts, 6 days a week—so I am utterly appreciative of their time and support.

Edible Houston's publisher and my friend Kim Korth always had my back. Without Kim, it would have been challenging to juggle the manuscript deadline and the scheduled issues for *Edible Houston*. Hugs to Cath Stewart for your support and friendship. Also, conversations with Christina Martinez, Catherine Manterola, Geralyn Graham, Natalie Jones, Jodie Jones Eisenhardt, Alice Levitt, Karen Lerner, and Kate McLean have been invaluable in helping me push forward.

Danielle Centoni (*Portland Cooks*) and Julien Perry (*Seattle Cooks*): thanks for listening and sharing your insights!

A huge thank you goes out to my kitchen crew: Nuala Ewins, Evelien Kleijn, Stephen Maclin, and Letitia Verlander.

Many thanks go out to the entire team at Figure 1 Publishing, including publisher Chris Labonté for believing Houston belongs in this series and editor Michelle Meade for her unwavering support and encouragement throughout the process. Her edits made me a better writer all around. Thank you also to eagle-eye editors Judy Phillips and Lucy Kenward for their tremendous work. And last but not least, thank you to the creative team—art director Naomi MacDougall, photographer Chris Brown, and prop stylist Tina Hunt—for capturing the creativity of our talented chefs. It was, in a word, awesome to work with all of you!

Finally, to my husband, Raymond Franssen, and my son, Mees, for being my sounding board, for the helpful conversations, for shaking the cocktails and pouring the wine, and for eating all those random meals on recipe-testing days.

Index

★ ★ ★

About the author

★ ★ ★

Francine Spiering is a food writer and blogger (lifeinthefoodlane.blog) with a degree from Le Cordon Bleu Paris. As the editor of *Edible Houston* and president of Slow Food Houston, she is committed to the city's local community and actively promotes the regional gastronomy through her work. She has also written for *The Boston Globe* and *Slow Food USA Eater's Digest*. Having lived on four different continents, she is a global citizen at heart. Francine lives in Houston with her husband, son, and dog. This is her first book.

The Series

Figure.1